AUTOBIOGRAPHY

OF

CHARLES HENRY POINTER

HIS LIFE HIS LEGACY

CHARLES HENRY POINTER

ISBN: 978-1-4669-6833-2 (sc)
ISBN: 978-1-4669-6832-5 (e)

Trafford rev. 06/17/2013

 www.trafford.com

North America & international
toll-free: 1 888 232 4444 (USA & Canada)
phone: 250 383 6864 ♦ fax: 812 355 4082

CONTENTS

FOREWORD

This book talks about my life experiences starting from the day I was born, March 12, 1950, to Silas and Lucy Pointer. Our family stayed in the Mill Creek area of St Louis, Mo., and later the Igoe projects. My mother raised two boys who later went on to graduate from college and made something of themselves and did not drift into a life of crime, drugs or gang life. I wrote about my boyhood, adolescent, and adult life and the happy and sad experiences I encountered as I grew into manhood, and the positive people I depended on for advice to overcome adversity, and the thrill of defeat and victory, when I accomplished my goals in my court battles as a Pro-Se litigant leading up to the United States Supreme Court, and winning five of more justices' votes to have my case placed on the docket, the 22nd Missouri Court of Appeals doing oral argument, and 24 cases in the 8th Circuit Federal Court, and many cases in the 8th Circuit Court of Appeals, and defeating 9 federal judges who signed an en banc order making me do eight unconstitutional measures, before I could file my cases in court, and I defeated them in the 8th Circuit Court of Appeals. I was a high school history and English teacher, a journalist writing for the newspapers, and a father. The overall book discusses the way that having faith in God helped me overcome the difficulty of achieving the setbacks which kept me from doing what I wanted to do to make a contribution to mankind.

I wrote how it hurt to be rejected by thirty law schools and the two local law schools; St.Louis University School of Law and Washington University School of Law, and after those defeats, I went to the University of Missouri and graduated cum laude and made the Dean's List. I went to paralegal school at Florissant Valley Community College and made the Dean's List and graduated cum laude and studied a year as a law student at Concord Law School, which is an online law school. I am the author of the book "The Making of a Black Belt Karate Champion" which shows how I won over 50 trophies in competition, a national championship, and two Gold Medals, two Bronze Medals, and two Silver Medals in the Missouri State Show Me State Games and started competing at the age of 42. However, I did not let my age stop me because the men I trained with were twenty years younger at the St. Louis Job Corps Center where I worked as a counselor, and counseled the students to avoid gangs, drugs, and a life of violent crime. I hope the readers of this book will be inspired to never give up their dreams to make something of themselves.

CHAPTER 1

HIS BIRTH AND EARLY BEGINNINGS IN LIFE

I was born on March 12, 1950 in St. Louis, MO to Silas and Lucy Pointer at Homer G Philips Hospital and my older brother Ronald in 1948 at the same medical facility. We lived on Spruce Street in the Mill Creek area of St. Louis in the early 1950's which consisted of a large African American populated community.

According to an article taken from the website, "Built St. Louis Web. Lug", the author indicated living conditions were considered unstable for the residents and the houses substandard needing indoor plumbing and many out houses were seen in their backyards. With that being the case, tragic events took place which led to the destruction of a striving community by the decision makers in powerful positions in St. Louis, Missouri with most of the houses needing repairs and upgrading. The deteriorating conditions forced civic leaders to destroy this community even though many of the residents who lived there owned businesses. The decision to demolish those dwellings, forced many thousands of African American dwellers in the Mill Creek Valley to move into eleven story high rise buildings located in the Pruitt and Igoe projects which were later torn down.

The article said the residents had a powerful network consisting of stores, restaurants, and other enterprises. Today large businesses such as A. G Edwards and other corporations are in that area and Harris Stowe University has built educational buildings and dormitories for their students to live in while attending the college.

As a child I remembered my father bringing hamburgers home for us to eat during his lunch period. Most of my life my mother raised me and my older brother. We did not grow up in a middle class neighborhood where many African Americans made their homes. Jefferson Street went in the direction of north and south down a hill and streets going east and west merged with it. There were black businesses on this street also. Today this area is an industrial park and rapidly growing with new businesses being developed with a vast railroad passing under the Jefferson Bridge going in an east and west direction. Located up the street was a toy factory which my brother and a group of his friends visited for fun to see what they could get into. On one such visit Ronald fell on some glass and was rushed to the hospital. My mother said Ronald kept kicking and screaming as the doctors sewed up his stomach. Sometimes at night during hot temperatures my father sweated and I remembered seeing beads of sweat forming on his head. Coming from the Southern states, Silas was African American and his body built small with light skin and he possessed a wonderful personality. When time permitted, my father took me and my brother to Mississippi and he told us about the small chickens we killed or messed with out of curiosity. Many black men experienced World War II, and I remember my mother telling us father was one of the lucky groups of service men who did not have to take part in the invasion of Japan because an American bomber dropped the atomic bomb on two cities in Japan destroying everything standing and killed thousands of people making Japan surrender to allied forces in 1945.

Dropping the bomb saved thousands of lives instead of losing more American soldiers invading the country. The thought of not invading Japan, because their government surrendered, made Silas very happy, and millions of other service men in my father's unit.

My father went to school under the GI bill and I remembered seeing one of the books he use to study with. Sometimes father took my brother and me to a movie located on Market Street not too far from Union Station where trains carried people to their destinations and we enjoyed eating candy and watching the movie. The picture was about the United States Marine Corps fighting the Japanese on the pacific islands they took when they invaded them and the star was Aldo Ray.

When I was seven years old in 1957, my mother moved into the Igoe projects. The Igoe projects stood 11 stories high and many people lived in the apartment building. My father came back to live with us while we stayed there. Sometimes my father and I rode our bicycles underneath the building and in an accident my handle bars hit a kid in the head and I ended up fighting his sister. To pay the bills, my mother worked at many jobs to take care of us.

Other employment landed my mother a job at the Mart Building where she met a teletype operator by the name of Herman Jackson, who she later married. Herman dressed and groomed himself and wore Stacy Adams shoes, and styled his well cut hair with waves, and he sported a mustache, and his built was well toned with muscles, and his height was at least 6 feet. Serving his country in the United States Marine Corps, Herman told me what it was like being a soldier and traveling to different countries. While staying in the projects, Ronald and I went to Blewett Elementary Grade School. I remembered having much fun growing up as a young child. To have fun, me and a group of boys started at the 11th floor of our apartment building and jumped all five steps without touching any of them landing on the base of the concrete floors at a rapid speed until we reached the first floor. At school my teacher did not consider me to be a great student and I failed to go on to the next level two times and be promoted. The failures only made me determined to become a better student in the future years of my life. I got discouraged at times but I felt I had to believe in God and keep on trying to accomplish the dreams I wanted to complete.

At that time in 1957 and 1958 students got beat with paddles or rattans to stop bad discipline and I was one of those who remembered a white teacher hitting me in front of the class with one of them. Our gym teacher used a wooden paddle on the boys when they got out of line. In many cases, the parents approved of such beatings. A fellow by the name of Donald Bright taught in the Dallas Public School System, and he told me they used the paddle on students in the high school, and elementary schools.

A couple of buildings down from our housing complex in the projects was an area built for kids to ride on swings and they glided at least 20 feet into the air. Two kids usually performed this activity when playing in the swings to see how high they could go never worrying if they got hurt.

Between the two rows of buildings were open grass fields where the boys played baseball, and people lounged on the grass, and in front of the buildings people sat on benches in the evening when the weather appeared to be nice.

Children getting hit by cars became a major problem when they crossed the street going to the supermarket. When different venders brought products to Gershawn's Market located across from 2250 Cass Avenue, the local thugs came from the projects and stole cases of sodas and beer off the trucks when drivers made deliveries to the store. They escaped by running across Cass Avenue and going into large eleven story buildings where it was easy to hide from the police who tried to catch them. Some of the children did not have shoes to wear, and it was apparent they grew up in poverty, and accepted it as a way of life.

When the weather appeared to be good, the Central Baptist Church bus came to the projects, and kids sat on the parked bus, and participated in singing gospel songs with church members. For local entertainment, my brother and I went to the movie theaters located on Franklin Avenue called the Criterion and the Roosevelt located west of that theater. During the summer months we went to the 10th street pool located further downtown and played in the cold water. Not too far from the 10th street pool, we ventured into a small neighborhood park where some white boys chased us back to the projects. As I remembered, we wanted to see what the other side of the park looked like, and this was my first experienced with racial prejudice. When going to school in the fifties, teachers used rattans and I remembered getting hit with one and the teachers in that time period did not have problems with student discipline like they do today.

I remember my gym teacher using a paddle for discipline and as he swung it in so many angles a person did not know where to move his hips to avoid getting hit. While my mother worked, we were supposed to stay in the apartment but Ronald disobeyed her and one day he was chased home by one of his fellow thug friends and he knocked on the door and shouted "Charles get the gun !" The problem here is there was no gun and big brother only wanted to scare him away.

Floyd Irons and his family lived in the 2250 Cass building and he went to Langston University and got his degree in history and later taught it at Vashon High School and became one of the coaches who won several Missouri state basketball championships. Darlene Green grew up in the housing projects at that time and graduated from Vashon High School and Washington University with a degree in Accounting and she became the first African American female to become elected comptroller for the city of St. Louis, MO, and I am proud to say she is my first cousin. My brother Ronald went to St. Louis University and earned a degree in Business Administration and grew up in the housing projects with me. Another good friend of mine by the name of Howard Miller spent his early life as a child in the housing projects and today he is Dr. Howard Junior Miller, and he taught as a college professor for 13 years. Many of the fellows staying in the projects ended up dead or were sent to prison for living a life of crime.

Deciding to leave the projects in the early 1960's, my mother moved to a street called Terry Avenue and she enrolled us in Laclede Grade School. Laclede was overcrowded and they bused many students from our school to Walbridge Grade School located on the north side of St. Louis populated by white students. There was no integration because all the white students were on one side of the building and the black students on the other. Our recesses and lunches started on different times from each other.

It was separate but equal because some of the black students asked why we could not socialize with the white students. "Mr. Ferracane, why are we segregated from the white students?" Donna Wells asked him one day. His response was, "You did not come over here to sleep with them." Mr. Ferracane was a nice teacher and taught us the best way that he could and I remember him dictating to us sentences and having us write them down on line paper. This assignment proved to be vital because it taught me to take notes down during my college lectures. The girls did better than the boys in math. When his students wanted to have a party, he let us have one and a dance called the Twist was popular at that time. For activities in the school yard, instead of playing baseball, the boys got into groups and had fist fights with each other just to see who was the toughest. In some cases serious injuries resulted from such rough play. Playing game sports was the activity we were supposed to be doing. When times were hard for my family, Mr. Farracane bought my lunch for me when I did not have any money to pay for it. Mr. Farracane loved playing baseball with the students. In 1960, my mother moved to a street called Union and this was a wide street with cars running at about 35 miles an hour. We lived in an apartment house above the store my mother worked at called Jamie's Package Liquor. Across the street was a public library and I got permission to go there and read books. This activity sparked my desire to be something in life because I read about famous people and what challenges they made to become successful in their lives. There was a fellow who lived a few doors from us by the name of Henry Dune and he came from the South who I played with. To have fun, the neighborhood boys took long narrow boards and nailed a clothespin on one end of it. At the other end was a rubber band. A soda top was placed in between the rubber band and stretched towards the clothes pin which held it. If you wanted to shoot someone you could. This was a popular game the young boys played with each other and many of the fellows stood on garage roofs shooting at you. It was a lot of fun but if you got hit with a soda bottle top the sting of it hurt. My brother Ronald and I worked a paper route while we lived on Union Avenue. Earning money took our interest and we never thought about child support nor did we receive it from our father.

In the early sixties, our family lived on Terry in a four family flat and my mother worked as a cook and did other jobs to take care of us. One of the albums I played was "Take Five" by Dave Brubeck. Jazz at the time was not as commercial as it is today. The majority of dwellings on Terry Avenue were four family flats with a lot of people living in them. A Jewish boy by the name of Joey Melee influenced me to read about educational topics. Joey and I owned chemistry sets and we did experiments which increased my reading comprehension. Coming from a strong Jewish background, Joey lived with his mother and grandmother. Joey's next door neighbor was a Caucasian and his name was Larry and having a glass eye made him want to prove he was tough. Adventure was something Joey loved and sometimes he and I traveled five miles from our house and went to Barret Brothers Park and near the outskirts of the railroad tracks rainwater flooded a patch of land that one day would be built into an apartment complex which is still there today. Acting as if we were pirates, we got some flat crates made of wood and floated them on water and tried to push each other off of them and after that we came home with mud on our clothes,

The street of Terry back in 1961 consisted of a row of four family flats going down a hill. Most of the people living on Terry were black. My brother's friends Bobby Collins and Poncho did not like me following them so I spent much time with Joey. To have fun, Joey and some of my brother's friends played Rebels and Yankees pretending to be fighting battles in the Civil War between the states.

One summer day, I broke into my grandfather's car and released the emergency brake and it rolled into an old garage and knocked it down. In the family flats, other families lived in two story apartments near 5863 Terry. My brother and his friends brought girls up to the house, played music, and danced to the music of Motown recording artists. As usual they did not want me in the living room with them. I should have charged them for not telling momma. (Smile)

We moved to 5620 Cates in 1962 or 1961 and I rode a bus to Laclede Elementary Grade School. One evening while I was standing in the front of a store, a young brother by the name of LC asked if I had some money and I said no. Later he saw me coming out of the store with my food and got angry because he felt I lied to him. Trying to show how tough he was LC took off his coat and we fought each other and later the fighting stopped. My mother came and escorted me back home after school officials called and told her about the incident and later I was transferred to another school.

When my family moved to 5620 Cates, it was an apartment building with twelve families living in it. The building's driveway went into the basement and the sides of it were surrounded by a lawn trampled down by children who came over to play with us. This was a period of my teen years when Motown Records was in its starting stages. I attended Hamilton Grade School located on Westminster Avenue. My eighth grade teacher Mrs. Pillow was Caucasian and I enjoyed her class. Mrs. Pillow showed us photos of the trips she and her husband Henry made to historical places in the United States.

One of her students by the name of Gentry Trotter wore his choir robe to class and singed gospel music. Arthur and I became good friends. Arthur's complexion was brownish in color and he weighed at least 185 pounds. Arthur and I joined the basketball team and played in tournaments together and he became top point man in scoring. Arthur's sister, Patsy attracted many boys who tried to court her because of her beautiful figure and pleasant personality. All of us attended Hamilton Elementary Grade School located on Westminster Avenue.

To take industrial arts, the whole class walked to a school located near Highway Forty and on the way back we traveled through Forest Park and enjoyed seeing different sites like the Art Museum, golf courses, and Jefferson Memorial which contained artifacts of the 17th and 18th century, like long rifles, Indian artifacts, clothing, farming, and hunting tools, and pictures of that period. One student by the name of Jimmy Mayes walked on the ice when he thought it would hold him and it did not, the ice broke and he fell in, but he managed to get out of it and became very cold as he traveled home. Sometimes Arthur and I liked fighting the boys with our fist but avoided hitting each other in the face but one day Charles Gravy hit me in the face several times saying he was sorry.

"Man we are going to get him back," Arthur said to me.

The next day Charles came out of the school yard and I hid on one side of the entrance and Arthur was on the other and when he came into the schoolyard we both attacked hitting him in his body and he dropped to the ground as he received more punishment. So much excitement took place that Charles did not know what hit him as Arthur and I ran away laughing. No hard feelings existed between Charles and me after he was paid back for breaking the rules of orderly combat. (Smile) We wanted to even the score and when he broke the rules; we made him pay for it because instead of Charles trying not to hit my face he did it on purpose.

Another person who lived several houses down the street became a great friend of mine by the name of Douglas Jones and his step-father and mother lived in Clovis, New Mexico. His step father's name was Tim and he served in the United States Air Force. Our conversations consisted of Doug talking about the foreign countries his family lived in and the state of Alaska.

"North to Alaska" was a song the kids sang when I stayed up there. Doug told me.

Light complexed and weighing about 150 pounds, Doug styled his hair like Smokey Robinson lead singer of the Miracles. The day I met Doug, he walked down the street, stopped and we spoke to each other. Our relationship lasted for the years, through high school, until I went to college in 1969.Doug's aunt and uncle lived in a four family flat. Martial Arts were one of Doug's hobbies and our relationship grew as he taught me karate. After school, I went to his aunt and uncle's apartment and trained in Doug's backyard doing kicks, punches, and blocks. Another friend of ours by the name of Carl Roper practiced with us. One evening a photographer came by and took pictures of

Doug and Carl sparring with each other in Forest Park. The pictures were beautiful but Doug did not want all of them showing Carl getting hit in the face.

"Keep on shooting!" Carl said as he and Doug kept throwing kicks and punches at each other. Doug was four years older than me, and he taught me many things about life I appreciate to this day. We enjoyed looking at karate films to see how the masters trained and did their katas. To earn income, Doug worked with his grandfather at a toy store in Kirkwood, MO. Before I started seeing girls, Doug taught me things about how to have a good conversation with them and some of the activities they liked doing. One evening Joe came to the house as we trained in Doug's back yard and he sparred with me and hit me in the face and bragged to the boys about it. "I sparred with Charles and beat him and he knows more than I do. "Joe told the boys.

Doug arranged for me to spar with Joe again and when I sparred with him again; he threw a front kick at me and I blocked it, and hit him in the mouth with a forward punch, and he followed with the same technique, and I blocked it and hit him in the neck with a shuto, which ended the fight. It was good to get revenge on him. Back in those days we walked where we wanted to go. Most of the time three boys went to see one girl.

To be in our group, being a good dancer was required when we went to court the girls. Doug taught me how to dance and what to say to the girls when trying to get a good understanding with them when problems came up. I grew up as a teenager during the sixties when Motown Records was in its heyday. Many of the artist thrilled us as we listened to their singers such as Marvin Gaye, Stevie Wonder, The Temptations, and Smokey Robinson and the Miracles, and The Supremes just to name a few of the many great recording artists at Motown in Detroit, Michigan.

Being inspired by their music, we formed a singing group consisting of Larry Liggins, James Smith, who we called Smithy, Doug, Iris, and me. Most of the songs we practiced were by the Miracles. Everything was ok until the boys flirted with Iris and the group broke up. Being young and teenagers we did not know what we really wanted to concentrate on.

As a younger person, I worked for the janitor cleaning the sidewalks and taking down the trashcans at our apartment building.

CHAPTER 2

O'FALLON TECHNICAL HIGH SCHOOL
1964 TO 1968

In 1964, I went to O'Fallon Technical High School and graduated in 1968. This was a time period when the civil rights movement occurred and I saw the evening television news reports showing black people sitting at lunch counters and angry white people threw food in their faces as they tried to get served, and their protest marches on the nation's highways by people from all races and creeds, because black people could not vote in the Southern states or go to places of public accommodations, but served in Vietnam and fought for their country. "Hell no we want go!" came shouts from the protesters on national television, showing young men burning up their draft cards to not fight in an undeclared war.

I remember when Dr. Martin Luther King was assassinated in Memphis, Tennessee; I read magazines articles on him which my mother brought home from the bookstore. The Vietnam War was part of our lives but I did not enlist in the service. Two students I knew who went to O'Fallon were killed in Vietnam. As the Vietnam War progressed the news media announced the number of soldiers killed in combat and it increased each day. As a student I majored in commercial art at the high school. I was never sent out to intern in a place of business where I could get the experience or any of the students who were in my class. I wrestled my freshmen year, football my second year, and tennis my senior year. During one football game, I let a boy run into the end zone after the other team was beating us 40 to 0. Some of my teammates thought I did this on purpose but he just out ran me trying to get the touch down. I met my old buddy Arthur on the football field and did not know he was out there playing on the opposing team. Arthur stayed down the street from me on Cates. The school Arthur played for was named Soldan High School. In the morning, Herman Shelton came by and picked my brother and me up to take us to school at O'Fallon Technical High School. My brother Ronald was on the varsity football team and played an outstanding four years as a linebacker. When I got into fights, he normally intervened and talked to the people I had conflicts with. One time Steve Bell pulled on my new shirt and I hit him. Steve being very tall in height felt he was tough. Big brother went and talked to him and the dispute ended. As an athlete, I played football, tennis, and wrestled.

My brother met his wife Sandra Martin at O'Fallon Tech in 1964. They grew very close, and every day he and Sandra caught the bus home together after school. They got married after graduating from High School and have been together ever since. They have two sons together.

Howard Miller and I met at O'Fallon Technical High School and we were in the Commercial Art Department, and he came from a big family, and grew up in a rough environment, and ghetto life got him involved with the wrong type of boys, and later he was sent to Booneville Reform School. While we attended high school, Howard worked at the Roosevelt Hotel. The football coach needed people to help with taking materials to the workers who placed white lines on the football field and Howard told me about it. Getting excited about what Howard told me, I went and asked coach could I help out. I wore nice looking clothes and a vest and students laughed at me when they noticed I pushed a wheel barrel at the same time. I got after Howard for tricking me into getting embarrassed for trying to make an honest dollar and all the women were laughing at me too. He still remained my old buddy. (Smile)

Howard tried out for the football team and broke his leg in the process. I took swimming lessons as part of gym and enjoyed doing it. One day I got ambitious and decided to try deep water and almost drowned and one of the students jumped into the water and pulled me out. Years later I met him at a shopping mall, and I did not know who he was, but he told me about the incident, and I thanked him again. When Howard and I were at O'Fallon Tech, we talked about our future and he said he wanted to attend college and run for elective office.

Outstanding leadership and organization qualities were things Howard developed as a gift. Writing compositions were something I enjoyed and the other liberal arts courses. In the art classes, we did different projects for three or four hours. Watercolor took my interest especially when I painted an old Mexican mission. When going to dances as freshmen, I was shy but when I got be to an upper classmen;

I went to the school dances. In our science classes, I remembered a student who said he was going to make some sparks in an experiment which lit up the class with laughter. It was difficult for him to explain what took place as the sparks kept hitting him in the face, and spreading to different sections of the laboratory, where we did our experiments. One of our instructors by the name of Mr. Uphouse talked about politics more than he did electricity. We knew what the Democrats and Republicans were doing after he spent most of the time speaking about their policies instead of electricity.

When I went to Forest Park Community College, Howard and I realized the civil rights movement was being studied by students at other high schools but not us. Many things in the liberal arts program were not taught by our teachers at O'Fallon Tech. Bad discipline was not a problem in the classes at O'Fallon and the boys and girls came to school dressed neatly as compared to the students of today. Wearing Afro's became popular in the 1960's. School spirit became strong when our teams won in different sports like basketball, track, and football. In basketball, our team won the 1968 state championship and the name of the school, O'Fallon Technical High School was changed to Gateway. I graduated in June of 1968, and made plans to attend college. The school prom came and Larry and I took our lady friends with us and enjoyed ourselves.

My mother and I had our usual problems during my teenage years and I did not like being cursed at, which made me run away to stay with Doug and his aunt. I got a job working at Peabody Coal Company coloring land maps. This was my first job after high school working downtown in a big building in front of the riverfront. Mr. Touhill hired me and he did legal work for the company.

While staying in Kirkwood, I met Augusta Moss and I guess she was my first love when I was 19 years of age. Her friends and family called her Gus. The secondary school Gus attended was Kirkwood High School and most of her friends were Caucasian. Two people Doug introduced to me were Mr. Jones who was black and a postman and Mr. Chiles an elderly white person with white hair who taught math at

Meramec Community College and I did not know what role they would play in my life but it became a positive experience. When we practiced karate together in Doug's back yard, Mr. Jones visited and watched us perform the different techniques. He was a postman and his children's names were Billy Junior and Gaynail. His son Billy and OC, his friend, worked on cars together, and competed with them in car races.

One trait Mr. Jones possessed was his ability to trust people. To supplement his salary, he owned a store, and waited on customers who were residents of Meachum Park. Realizing he could not be there because of postal duties required by his job, Mr. Jones left his door open and allowed people to come in and buy what they wanted when he was gone. The customers left their money and wrote a list of what they bought. When coming to Mr. Jones's ranch house, you saw artwork he did hanging on the walls. His daughter Gaynail was a journalism student and sometimes I spoke to her when I called Mr. Jones about a particular social problem I experienced. When I applied for college, Mr. Chiles enrolled me in a figure drawing class.

"Charles, I am going to get you a job and Mr. Chiles will get you registered for college," Mr. Jones told me. One evening I called and spoke to Mrs. Chiles 'wife who displayed a friendly attitude when she answered the telephone. Mr. Chiles' first name was Truman and Mr. Jones 'first name was William. Both of them are deceased now. Mr. Jones studied physical therapy while he was in college but he said there were no jobs for black people in the field when he majored in it during the fifties because of discrimination during that time period. Sometimes Mr. Jones and Billy practiced martial arts together. Meachum Park consisted of a community with 100% black citizens, but it was time to adjust to being out on my own, and to my new environment. I ran away from home trying to get from parental authority, but ended up going to school at night, and taking figure drawing.

All the art classes were filled up but Mr. Chiles enrolled me into a class, and paid for it himself, and bought my supplies, and I paid him back. Doug and I moved to his Aunt Mattie's house, and she was in her eighties at the time and lived in an area called Meachum Park, a low income area of black home owners. Early in the morning Doug and I got up and took a bus ride to Bemis Bags located in Fenton, Missouri. The bag company was very big and they made a lot of burlap and paper bags. A fellow by the name of Peter influenced me to get my degree because he graduated from a black college and he became a manager trainee at the company.

Being my counselors, Mr. Jones and Mr. Chiles spoke to me about my problems and became wonderful friends and the company where Mr. Jones got me a job was very big and hired many people. The workforce at the bag company consisted of mixed racial groups of people. Doug worked in the department which packed the bags and I was in the printing department and my responsibilities were to get ink for the pressmen to complete their assignments. The supervisor Jim Oliver and I did not get alone at times, and debated much about company policy. My title was Ink Man, and by the end of the work day ink appeared all over my clothes, and it was then I realized I did not want to do this type of work all of my life. When it came to measuring the ink for print jobs, an engineer helped by showing me how I could provide the right amount of ink so they could finish their ink printing jobs. By having a high school education it was important to me, but some people like Dan did not like the fact an African American male graduated from high school, and attended college. Regardless of what I attempted to do, Dan did not like me. I realized black people would hurt you just like white people could. Many times I complained about the way Dan treated me.

"Pointer, you're not doing this job right"! Dan always shouted at me. Eventually Mr. Jones intervened and spoke to company officials and Dan stopped harassing me. My mother worried about me and wanted to know what type of life style I was living in Kirkwood, MO. Her thoughts were relieved because Mr. Chiles called and told her where I stayed and she came out to the house and persuaded me to come back home.

"Charles you can come back home and go to school." My mother said to me.

I thought about what she said and wanted to get away from the bag company, and being dirty with ink on my clothes all day. I went back home to stay with my mother and finished my figure drawing course and received a grade of c. Going back home was a hard decision for me to make but I wanted to complete college.

CHAPTER 3

FOREST PARK COMMUNITY COLLEGE
1969 TO 1971

My experience at Forest Park Community College located in St. Louis, MO started in January of 1969. My school life was exciting at the age of 19 and a single male. I joined the college choir and judo team. The thought of learning how to throw people was fun. Our instructor's name was Sensei Laud and he disciplined his students in an excellent manner. Under Sensei Laud, we learned the one arm shoulder throw, the hip throw, inner reaping throw, outer reaping, and two arm shoulder throw.

Grappling techniques gave us the ability to choke people on the ground or standing up. One day Bob Ford pulled on me and wanted to rondure before practice, which made Sensei angry, and he made us do pushups most of the class time. Rondure is when one person tries to throw the other person and the other person uses resistance to keep you from throwing him. The judo team went to various places to participate in competition against other judo schools. After two years of being on the club, I was promoted to a brown belt. Some humorous events took place when two boys practiced with each other and I attempted to give them directions on how they could improve their throws, and one of them said, "Why don't you come up here and show us how it is done."

Knowing I was the type of person who would not turn down a fight or challenge, I came out on the mat and fought one of the fellows. I held him tightly and rolled back and I placed my foot in his stomach and he went flying over me and hit the mat. When Sensei Laud gave a judo tournament at Forest Park Community College, I took part in it winning my matches, and placed first place in a judo tournament at Bellville Community College. It was fun going to the tournament with my teammates. At first, I enrolled in the art program but changed to liberal arts because of the prejudice shown by the art instructors. I took Figure Drawing 11, Drawing 1, Design 1, Lettering and Layout, and Introduction to Art, and Art Appreciation.

My counselor, Tom Curtiss said to me, "Why keep taking these art classes if you feel you are not getting fair grades in this subject area". I took classes in choir and class voice under him. By January of 1969, Howard Miller my old high school friend was a student at Forest Park Community College. To get adjusted to college life, Howard enrolled in the general curriculum program. I did not take courses which prepared me for college work. The field of liberal arts appealed to Howard and that was a transfer program to a four year program.

"You ought to go into the liberal arts program because you cannot measure how they are evaluating your art." Howard said to me. After listening to Howard, I decided enrolled into the liberal arts program. I took courses in the humanities, social sciences, physical education, sciences, and math areas. I enjoyed my history and English classes the most. Papers on the killings at Meli, South Vietnam and the Yalta Conference were written about by me.

Campus unrest resulted when black student groups played Malcolm X's album in the cafeteria and the college president stopped them, which caused a riot when campus police tried to keep them from doing this activity. This was a time during the civil rights period and I remembered reading in the college newspaper at Forest Park Community College some students protested against the Vietnam War by pulling down the flag, and during that same time period, students at Washington University set the ROTC building on fire. I felt we should not have got involved in that war.

When I attended Forest Park Community College, I joined the college choir under the direction of Dr. Tom Curtis. He divided the group into tenors, basses, altos and sopranos and passed out music for us to learn. It was mostly European music and Mr. Curtis 'wife practiced with all four ranges of those voice groups in our choir. For example, the basses singed their part of the song and the tenors, altos, and sopranos were alerted when to sing their sections of the music, when Mr. Curtis waved his hand back and forth for them to sing.

I wondered how we learned all that music but when the concert started we were ready to perform and we never let him down.

While at Forest Park Community College, I pledged a fraternity called Alpha Phi Alpha. The Alpha people told me to be at an apartment complex called Alpha Gardens and at a certain address. I did not know what to expect but I showed up anyway to meet my new pledge brothers.

The fraternity stressed brotherhood and your little brothers were supposed to dress the same but we did not know it. On that morning, Tim, a Washington University student majoring in engineering, showed up and he was light complexed and weighed about 230 pounds and played football for the university. His hair was long, curly, and black and he wore blue jeans and tennis shoes.

James was also light complexed and he became president of the group, and he attended St. Louis University, and he was slightly built. James' major was business administration, and Bruce became a pledge brother, and he attended St. Louis University, and lived on the city's North side with his father and mother. His father made a living installing windows into buildings and houses. Bruce's height was about 5'9" and he weighed about 200 pounds possessing a muscular built.

A slim person by the name of George Gross pledged with us and he weighed about 150 pounds and wore a large afro hair style. George told us what to expect from the big brothers when trying to be admitted into the fraternity.

Everyone showed up at the meeting except our Dean of Pledges and the Big Brothers gave us a royal ridiculing because most of us came to the meeting dressed in different types of clothes. Our Dean of Pledges was not there to protect the new pledges before going to the meeting, and did not meet with us to explain what we were suppose to wear, to show unity and brotherhood. When there was a meeting, all the pledge brothers were suppose to wear the same uniforms. One main requirement was to learn the history of the fraternity and if you did not know it; they punished you. Another requirement they wanted us to do was call them on the phone and get to know all the members of the fraternity. This was important because those individuals would make a decision to vote on you to become a member of Alpha Phi Alpha. We gave lawn parties to raise money, and if a big brother asked you to bring him a girl; she better be pretty, and possess an outstanding figure. If you did not do what he told you to do, you paid the price at the next pledge meeting with strict punishment. One thing I can say is they made me do things I thought I could never do, and I learned how to think under pressure, and memorize facts, about the history of Alpha and repeat them when they were getting you high off of wine or beer, or made you smoke cigarettes.

If they found out you did not drink, they got you drunk. If one of your brothers did not know the history of the fraternity the other members of the pledge group paid for it with strict punishment given out by the big brothers. Many of the Big Brothers made you make pillows for them and sent many of us on errands to buy things for them. The big brothers kept you busy but new pledges had to keep a C average in your overall grade point to get into the fraternity. I made all of my grades and felt it would be no problem getting into the frat because I called the big brothers up and did everything I was supposed to do. Our dress was the following: A yellow short sleeve shirt, a black and gold sphinx head and black slacks. To make money for our different activities, we gave lawn parties. That was during the summer and one of James Brown's hottest bestselling records at that time was a song called "Hot Pants." Many of the girls attending those parties wore shorts which came up to their thighs because it was summer and the weather was hot. I remember when we played the big brothers in a game of softball, and it was five of us, and 15 of them. No matter how many runs we got our score was always lower than theirs and we felt they were cheating us when we made homeruns.

One night the frat brothers took us to O'Fallon Park and we played touch football running up a 100 foot hill and they gave us a grand beating but we stuck together and made it safely home. After one pledge meeting, they made us drink some Mad Dog wine, and everyone got drunk. James realized this and stopped the car and we went to sleep for several hours. James and I went to a meeting without our pledge brothers, and the big brothers gave us a beating for it and said, "You do not come to a meeting without your pledge brothers."

When hell week came, none of the brothers decided to take part in it. I would have gone but I was not going to go without my pledge brothers. I later heard the fraternity had a meeting and they voted and I was the only one who made it but since the other pledge brothers and myself did not attend hell week I could not become an Alpha. Even now I feel like making a protest to the general Alpha Pi Alpha fraternity about this.

Howard formed a group called the Highlights and it consisted of four members. There was a concert being given at Wohls Center located on Dr. Martin Luther King Drive and Kings Highway. This was a big recreational building with a large swimming pool and gym and smaller rooms for civic functions. News got around there was a concert being held at the place and Howard felt the Highlights could take first place. The group members attended the rehearsals except Theodis known as Goldie. Today his name is Wali because he is Muslim. The group members felt Goldie should not have joined them for the concert because he never came to practice and they did not like his voice quality. The group decided not to tell Goldie about the concert. On the day of the concert all the members were there to give the greatest concert of their singing career and the singers were shocked when Goldie showed up with his uniform on ready to sing with them. He did not know what songs they were going to sing or what dance steps the group was going to do. As the Highlights came up to the mike to sing the crowd went wild and started clapping because they singed a song called," You Got the Power of Love Girl." The boys got down that night and every time Goldie sang Howard kept grabbing the microphone trying to please the crowd. After that concert the group retired from singing.

Many events took place because the boys were young and in their early twenties just two years out of high school and maturity was not a major goal developed at that time in their lives. All of them wanted to be stars and college students at the same time.

One evening I went out to the park with a student named Ollie and we sat on the grass talked and enjoyed each other's company. I told Howard I met a nice young lady when I saw him again.

Howard said, "How did the girl look?"

I said, "Man she was built with pretty brown skin and when she looked at you; she always presented a sexy smile."

As I described her features and the clothes she wore Howard said," Man that's my women and chased me around the park playing. As a student at Forest Park Community College, I participated in the college work-study program located at Wohl Center and team sports such as basketball. At the same time I received a grant and got an apartment on Delmar. I attended college during the day and worked four hours in the evening until about 10 o'clock at night. When I came home, I was tired but I stayed up much later studying until I went to sleep. For a year, I worked in TV Control at Forest Park Community College, where I was part of a television crew, who took part in video tapping guest speakers appearing on campus.

Howard wanted to become a social worker as a major career objective. In June of 1971, Howard and I embarked on a crusade to transfer to a four year college, and Howard master minded the project.

Howard said," Charles lets apply to many colleges and scholarship organizations. We might get lucky and win a scholarship. By the way let's apply for a Danforth Fellowship."

After sending in my application for the Danforth Fellowship, I received correspondence at my apartment telling me to go to Washington University and have a talk with an administrator who said once I arrived," Charles why are your grades so low ?"

I said, "I ran into a lot of prejudice in the art department and I deserved better grades than that."

He said," What do you want to do after you get out of college?"

I relaxed and said," I would like to write about events occurring in society," and showed him my essay which was published by Bemis Story a company magazine. I did not think much about the interview because I focused on other things like trying to graduate and get my first Associate of Arts degree. Sometimes I called Mr. Chiles and complained about the way I was treated by the art professors but he told me to keep on trying. I did not like the grading because they did not have a standard procedure on how they graded your work. Going into liberal arts changed my whole perspective of how I viewed life and taking courses in United States history, western civilization, art appreciation, English composition, Biology 1 and 11, and American and English literature shaped my way of thinking about the world. I remember writing a paper on the Meli massacre where some American soldiers raided a Vietnamese village and killed men, women, and children.

In my American history class, I wrote a paper on the Yalta Conference and Dr. Nolan was the professor. I explored how the allies divided up Germany after the war ended. I never realized World War II ended twenty three years earlier after I wrote that paper. I was a baby boomer born in 1950 five years after World War II ended.

As I studied my lessons, Howard called and said he won the Danforth Fellowship and I was happy for him. The fellowship paid for his degree program at the University of Missouri, St. Louis, MO in the area of sociology and a Master of Social Work graduate program at Washington University, St. Louis, MO. Howard specialized in community development when taking his coursework at Washington University. Still full of ambition, Howard earned his PHD in higher education and for 13 years taught on the college level.

Both of us mailed letters to colleges and scholarship foundations and I received many rejection letters. An application and scholarship form was filled out by me and mailed to Southern Illinois University at Edwardsville and I patiently waited for a reply.

One of the areas of concern Howard brought to me was the following when he said: "Charles I won the Danforth Fellowship because I wanted to work in the community on civic problems and you wanted to write about them."

When I was a high school student at O'Fallon Technical High School, the Plumbing Industry sponsored an essay contest called "Speak Up For America" in 1968 and I entered it. The essay dealt with our involvement in the Vietnam War. When I attended Forest Park Community College, the company I worked for called Bemis Bags published the essay in their company magazine called "Bemis Story", which inspired me to take more courses in English at the community college.

While I was a student at Forest Park Community College, I rode the bus to Kirkwood, Missouri to see Gus every weekend. She met a fellow at Meramec Community College who had a car and left me for him. He was light skinned and had curly hair. I could not compete with him because he could take her out and I could not afford to have a car to do the same things to make her happy. He really did me a favor because Gus became pregnant by the fellow, and years later after I graduated from college; she told me he had too many girlfriends. In a way, I am glad I was not the father, because I would have to stop college and get a job. On a visit out to her house in attempts of getting her back; I told them I would graduate, and finish college, and left the both of them in the door way, and walked twenty miles from her house to St. Louis MO; I could not catch the bus because it stopped running that late part of the evening. When I taught at Cleveland High School, I had a student in my class whose sister was a friend of Gus. When Gus visited his sister, they mentioned my name and my student asked her," "Do you know a Mr. Pointer?" Gus said, "Yes I went to school with him." Years later I met Gus again and told her I earned my Master of Science degree. She gave me her phone number when I saw her and girlfriends at a shopping mall, and that information was shared with her in a telephone conversation.

I was glad this real life situation took place because I made my promise to Gus and her boyfriend that I would complete college and graduate regardless of growing up in the low income areas I lived in. In my opinion, it's not where you come from, it's where you are going to improve your status and make a contribution to mankind. I did not let my race, which was black; stand in the way because professionals would have to accept me as I was. I was proud to be African American trying to overcome the hurdles which were thrown at me, to keep me from getting six degrees and a specialized certificate, from top ranked major colleges in Missouri and Illinois.

After two years of study, I was nearing the completion of my Associate of Arts degree and scheduled to graduate on June 7th 1971. I was 21 years old and this was a beautiful sunny day for this special occasion. My brother, mother, grandmother, and Mr. Chiles attended and we ate dinner at Mr. Chiles' home in Kirkwood, Missouri. My grandmother Fannie Green inspired me as well as my mother Mrs. Lucy Winfield, who disciplined me to the point where I wanted to be the best at what I was doing. I did not like the way I was spoken to with all the curse words my mother used in disciplining two boys, but she worked on many low skilled paying jobs to take care of her two boys, and we never knew what it was like to be hungry. We received Christmas toys and did many family activities together. At the time I was too young to understand the strict discipline my mother instilled in us, but it paid off because my brother and I never developed a police record as young kids growing up, and we both wanted to get good jobs, and be independent following our own careers. Raising boys in a family without the father can be difficult for a mother, but she showed much love and devotion in achieving this goal, to see her two sons graduate from college. Many of the boys we grew up with got sent to prison for a variety of crimes and my mother did not want us to end up like that.

I remember Howard saying to me", Charles your mother was rough on you but look at what it did for you, because she put fear in your heart not to get in drugs and crime, and you went on a positive journey and graduated from college."

My grandmother always encouraged me to keep on studying and one day she said going to school would pay off for me. By going to school and majoring in English and journalism helped me to write many court briefs, my college writing paper assignments, articles, and books. I remembered when my grandmother called me and said," How are you doing?"

I said, "I am studying my lessons."

She replied, "I see you are working your mind as usual," Grandmother was instrumental in getting us to attend the church where she was a member called Lively Stone Church of God in Christ.

The experience of getting my Associate of Arts degree tested my will power to accept the challenge of attending college and taking courses I did not have at O'Fallon Technical High School. At O'Fallon, I majored in commercial art and I did not take courses that were college prep. There is an old saying if you want something bad enough you must pay the price to get it, and I accepted the challenges that came my way.

I learned to socialize with different races of people when I attended this community college. During the summers participating in the work-study program at inner city schools in the low income parts of North St. Louis, I saw black people's children who were underfed and needed good role models to follow, and many of them were glad to see we were college students and most of the workers lived in their community. At many of the sites food sandwiches were handed out to kids who needed to be fed.

As a student at Forest Park Community College, I did not have the internet, and the use of lab tops like they do now, and most of the materials to write our papers came from getting books in the library. I attended Forest Park Community College from 1969 to 1971 and there was so much civil rights and social activities going on in the United States. If you tried to study at the school library, it became difficult because there were too many students in it, and often overcrowded with students doing research, and studying materials from courses they were taking. I discovered what it was like to study in classes during the day and working from 5 p.m. to 8.p.m. and studying from 10 p.m.in the evening to 3 a.m.in the morning. Now, I faced trying to figure out how I would pay for my education at a four year college institution and I wondered if my prayers would be answered by one of the institutions I sent a request for a scholarship if possible.

While I was a student at Forest Park Community College, I traveled by bus to see my father who stayed on Hickory Avenue located on the Southside of St. Louis. When I was younger, I could not visit my father, but when I got older I did, and developed a positive relationship with him. I worked at the tavern down the street from his apartment cleaning it, to make money for college expenses. Amos the owner said I could clean his tavern, and I did this and it helped me buy school clothes, and a bus pass for transportation to school. My father's friend Prince, who was elderly, served with General George Patton's army in Europe, and he often said, "That General Patton always wanted to go to the front." Years later my father died of throat cancer. My father's brother Uncle Johnny and his wife May treated me and my brother in a special way, and May encouraged me to keep on working to achieve my goals in whatever I did. I got a chance to teach Eric who was one of the sons of Uncle Johnny's daughters at Jennings Junior High, when I did substitute teaching at the school. Eric's occupation consisted of driving a bus for several years. For nearly thirty years, I did not know where my daughter Michelle was, but she contacted Eric and asked about me and later after talking to Eric I got a chance to meet her.

CHAPTER 4

SOUTHERN ILLINOIS UNIVERSITY AT EDWARDSVILLE, ILLINOIS 1971 TO 1974

In Becoming a Teacher of English and Social Studies

It was June of 1971 and I had not heard from any of the organizations I sent letters to. During the summer of June 1971, I worked for the Sewer Department and helped clean places like River Depere where sewage water flowed or we cut down weeds in various vacant lots and they lifted workers down into sewers to collect trash. After eight hours of working in the hot sun, I went to school at night taking a sociology class and I passed it with a grade of c. Mr. Chiles tried to help me get into Webster College, but they would not admit me. Years later I took paralegal classes at that college with no problems. I discovered what it was like to study in classes during the day and study from 10.p.m. to 3.a.m in the morning. Now I faced trying to figure out how I would pay for my education at a four year college, and I wondered if my prayers would be answered by one of the educational institutions I sent requests for a scholarship which would come through for me.

Out of curiosity, I went to SIU to see if I received a scholarship to that college because I filled out an application for one. I did not have any money or prospects of getting into college, but I felt opportunities would break for me. One thing I was happy about was not attending college and getting females pregnant. I wanted to go to school full time and finish in two years.

I enrolled in Southern Illinois University and did not hear from the scholarship committee and decided to go up there on the last day of registration and I did not have any money or prospects of getting into a four year college but I felt some opportunities would open up for me. Catching the bus in St. Louis, I traveled to Edwardsville, Illinois and I felt I had nothing to lose by going to see if I received any scholarships I applied for. It was September 1971 and I remembered the long ride to SIU and saw large cornfields as the bus traveled up the road to campus. The buildings on campus were mostly built with red bricks and as you entered the campus in your car there was a sign with about four or five languages welcoming you to SIU.

On the bus, I spoke to a fellow and I said, "Hi, my name is Charles and I am trying to enroll in the university and where are you from?"

He said," I am from South Africa and I am going to school up here."

I said to him, "I hope they will resolve their problems in that country."

He said," One day living conditions will be much better."

When Nelson Mandela was elected the first African president of that country, after years of uprisings, violence, and bloodshed between blacks and white citizens of that country, I saw black citizens were given the right to vote; I thought about what that fellow from South Africa said to me on our bus ride to SIU to attend the university back in 1971.

There were many people visiting the scholarship office trying to see if they received a scholarship and I was one of them. When I entered the office of the person who handled the scholarships, I asked him a question as I walked into his office and said, "I filled out a scholarship card but I did not receive a rely," and he said, "One card was sent to this address."

I looked at the document and it indicated school officials sent my scholarship card to an old address of mine. When I found this out, I called Howard and said," I got a scholarship to SIU!" I shouted through the phone.

"Man that's alright. Now go up there and make something of yourself!"

I said to myself success is a journey not a destination. After working so hard to complete my community college experience I said to myself, "I have arrived and I will get my degree."

Mr. Chiles and Mr. Jones were happy for me. The both of them saw a young black man with the help of God overcome the hardships of life, and go to a four year college called Southern Illinois University, at Edwardsville in September of 1971.

Donald Williams, one of the big brothers of the Alpha phi Alpha Fraternity, was a student up there also. He called himself Don Juan Williams, was African American, and he weighed about 149 pounds, and he wore an Afro hair style, and sported a beard, but it was neatly cut. I did not know what to major in so I spoke with my advisor Mr. Ware. Today Donald is an attorney with a family law practice.

I said, "I might want to go into journalism and become a writer but I fear having to learn how to type. I do not know what career objectives I would accomplish at the University. I first thought about completing the rest of my general studies courses first."

My mother bought me a bus pass each week to go up to the university but having money to spend was impossible without a job and very difficult having fun for recreational activities, and trying to get my degree at the same time, and when it came to getting girls for dates; it was impossible. Most of the girls wanted fellows who had jobs and a car to take them out on dates. Regardless of the setbacks, I was at a four year college institution, but I did not realize how difficult it would be to graduate from Southern Illinois University at Edwardsville. I was not going to stop going to college to take girls out. They had to accept me as I was or not at all.

I took a course called Healthful Living and I learned about keeping a healthy body. Having no good background in Earth Science proved to be challenging which I put on pass-fail. I spent ten weeks studying something I had no interest in. It was difficult studying about the ocean or altitudes and the formation on volcanoes, and the stars in the sky which I could not relate to. As I matured, I realized the best way to study courses in science was to have hands on experimentation. I remember taking Biology 11 in genetics, and I did not realize you have to have experiments, and test results, to understand what you were doing. I studied hard to pass Earth Science and I got a pass. I was from the hood and trying to understand what was happening in my community was difficult enough, and I could not relate to the earth and ocean and space sciences. Every day I left this class with headaches trying to understand what the professor was trying to teach. The next class I took was General Psychology 1 and there were maybe a hundred students taking it in the big lecture hall. My professor Dr. Robins did not know my name or me because there were about three hundred students taking his course. I placed the psychology class on pass-fail and after completing those two courses; I decided to become a teacher majoring in history and minoring in English in the secondary education program.

One of the professors who influenced me was Wilbur MacAfee, and he taught black history, and probably was in his sixties at the time he taught me. He was the first African American professor who taught me as an instructor. Professor MacAfee came from a black college and he told us he left that college because their president did not want them to protest against his policies. Professor MacAfee said to me," Charles if you attended a black college your grades would be much higher." It was a joy going into Professor MacAfee's office to speak with him. These talks in his office motivated me. From his lectures, I learned about black history and the challenges our people went through, to contribute something to American history, and America itself. One thing I remembered is he was the only African American who taught me as an undergraduate student. His complexion was a light brown skin and he had a thick black mustache. Before coming to SIU, he taught at an Afro American college. Professor MacAfee's lectures started with the African slaves being brought from West Africa. The rich kingdoms of Mali, Songhai, and Ghana were discussed also. As he walked back and forth across his classroom floor he said, "Most of your descendants came from West Africa. The slave catchers came to that region to get slaves to work in the plantations because they were skilled workers."

After class, me and some of the other students came into his office and spoke with him about black history and life in general. If any black students looked for a role model, they found it in him. He said positive things about the white instructors such as, "Some of them attempted to help the black students who were behind in their studies."

Another professor I remembered was Dr. Chen, who taught Chinese history, and his lectures consisted of the early developments of the Chinese culture, and how they grew into a great empire, and at the same time he worked on his PHD. He said to me, "Your English professor helped you by making you spend so much time in the writing lab."

Trying to pass Dr. Grant's classes became a problem and he asked difficult questions which seemed simple like: What is a Jew or Arab? Usually he wanted three or four pages to a question. The only problem I experienced was trying to understand what he wanted in the essay answer. I did not do well on his exams but received better grades under other instructors. Studying about the history of Rome, Dr. Santoni taught us Rome's army was one of the largest in the world, and its empire spread from England to the Middle East, and Rome defeated the other provinces, and united all the tribes into one nation. Dr. Santoni said the Romans trained their soldiers with perfection, and if they lost 200 men in battle; they replaced them in a matter of days.

One of my professors whose name was, Dr. Herbert Rosenthal, taught writing and Advanced American history. These events surrounding the late 1890's became the industrial age and Dr. Rosenthal taught with much enthusiasm. As he spoke to the other students in his class he said," I want all of you to select a thesis and pick a topic yourself."

When I was in his office, Dr. Rosenthal said, "Pick a topic you will enjoy."

Then he stated, "Charles why don't you do something on Stokely Carmichael?"

I said, "Who is Stokely Carmichael and what did he do?"

Dr. Rosenthal said," He was black civil rights leader who formed a group of people from southern, and northern cities, and towns trying to get equality for black people, so they could vote, and be given equal access to hotel accommodations and equal rights, to attend schools of their choice, and other things they could not enjoy before the 1964 Civil Rights Bill was passed."

After Dr. Rosenthal told me about Stokely, I did my thesis on him. In 1973, the internet was not discovered and most research projects were done by looking up books on the topic; I wanted to get information from. I gathered information and wrote page after page, but Dr. Rosenthal would not accept what I was writing because it was not organized.

"Charles I want you to develop an outline like this: Stokely's Early Life, Stokely's College Career, Stokely's Activities In SNCC (Student Non-violent Coordinating Committee) and After He Left SNCC"

Dr. Rosenthal said," Now when you find information pertaining to each section of your outline put it in those sections of the paper. You have too many unrelated topics in your paper."

"Thank you Dr. Rosenthal I will follow your directives," I told him. Researching about Stokely was very exciting and I learned about the civil rights period and how black and white students worked to register the field hands to vote in the southern states, and encouraged them to stand up for their rights which were denied them. In the research, I saw where they performed role modeling and students acted as if they were eating at a restaurant and other student's poured water and ice cream over their heads and called them ugly names to see if they could control themselves and not fight back. The principles of non-violence were used by that organization.

The research showed many of the white activist had better clerical skills than the black workers which caused many heated arguments and especially when black and white workers dated each other. The research indicated SNCC workers influenced the election results in different southern towns. The SNCC workers dressed in the same clothing as the field hands and spent more time with them than the organization formed by Dr. Martin Luther King. They spoke the field hand's language, and helped to get them organized, to register and vote to influence county elections, and elect the people who would make life better for them. It took a lot of hard work, but I completed the thesis on Stokely. The term Black Power originated from Stokely and what he meant was for black people to control their own destiny, and build an economic base power. Stokely felt if black people elected their own representatives; they could get better living conditions for their people, and challenge the Jim Crow laws, which were still in operation in the North and Southern parts of the United States. The research showed Stokely developed Pan Africanism whereas blacks in America would unite for a common cause and fight for equality over here and elsewhere in the world.

Stokely was educated at Howard University and earned his degree in philosophy. It was at Howard where he studied the great philosophies of Carl Marx, Dr. Martin Luther King, and Ghandi. I got a chance to meet Stokely when he visited Washington University to speak. He encouraged the students to fight for equality and never stop doing it. After his speech, I went back in a room where he talked to students.

As I approached Stokely, I held out my hand and shook his and said, "My name is Charles Pointer and I did my thesis on you. I spent hours studying about your life, philosophy, and your activities in SNCC."

Stokely smiled and said, "That was great and I hope you learned a lot about the struggles in our fight for equal rights for our people."

Looking at his surroundings, Stokely felt someone wanted to kill him. The sight of fear could be seen on his face as people approached to shake his hand.

I attended SIU from 1971 to 1975 during the civil rights period and much unrest took place between white and black students on campus. A year before I arrived, I saw a picture of the Illinois National Guard patrolling on campus to stop students from getting into a riot because of tension between white and black students.

Being black and attending SIU, I faced bigotry and discrimination from some of my white instructors, but as a whole many of them graded me fairly. I dearly loved Dr. Rosenthal who tried his best to help me with my thesis and I earned a B for my grade.

With many students coming from the inner city, some white professors made up their minds that black students were inferior to white students especially the ones in the English Department. Black students in many cases spoke black slang and dialect. Many of the black students on campus lived in the black community where standard English is not spoken. Most of the black students lived in the low income areas of East Saint Louis, Illinois.

I took a minor in English courses at Forest Park Community College because the professors taught it with a lot of fun and I liked the way they made you enjoy it. At SIUE taking English became a nightmare and I received low grades from four white English professors because they had a bias attitude about black students being able to become good English students.

One of the white English professors said," Charles you are a senior and maybe your professors passed you because you had a great personality."

I took my second English literature class from Dr. Slattery and I received low grades from him and wanted to drop his class. I did not like the way he taught because he wanted you to read 400 sonnets from the English writers and he placed twenty of them on a piece of paper and expected for you to know who wrote them. I felt he was crazy because all the sonnets sounded a like.

When I took English literature at Forest Park Community College, we studied the sonnets and discussed them and I enjoyed that. Being in Dr. Slattery's class bothered me because there were no black students in most of the English courses I took. There was no one I could study with or relate to. As Dr. Slattery approached the room to his class, it was just starting and I waited outside and spoke to him and he said, "Mr. Pointer why are you not going into the class room?"

I said," I do not need this class. I took an English literature course at Forest Park Community College and that met the satisfaction requirements for my minor in English at this university."

He said, "You can withdraw from this class on one condition."

I looked at him with a smile and he said, "You will have to write about 10 compositions on any topic that you want."

Even though I did not want to go to the writing lab to get out of his class ;I would do anything to not get a failing grade from him because I was not doing good in his class anyway. I do not think Dr. Slattery read the compositions but actually he was doing me a favor because writing is very important when communicating with people. I just did not like the way he taught this class.

Another major battle took place when I dropped English linguistics several times. I needed that course to complete my minor. Transformational Grammar was foreign to me, and it was a hurdle I would have to jump over after dropping the course several times. An African American student told me to take professor Ware who was working on his PHD for that course and I might pass it. This was subject matter I would not use in my professional life but it was required for graduation. My test scores were low and Mr. Ware later sent me a letter stating he could not pass me. I already walked across the stage for graduation and to fix the problem he told me to get tutoring in that subject matter and he would give me the test again. I went to his office and he said," I decided not to pass you. If you come back and get tutoring in the PS rules and take the test again we might be able to work things out so you can graduate."

Tears came to my eyes because I needed a job badly but I had no other choice but to do exactly what he wanted me to do in order to graduate and make money teaching in a school district.

This was the fall of 1973 and I said," I've been here for two years and I need a job badly but if it takes that to graduate I'll do it to get my degree."

By holding up my grade, my Bachelor of Science degree displayed 1974 instead of 1973. I received tutoring in the writing lab on

Transformational Grammar for ten weeks and learned a lot. I told my mother, brother, and grandmother about having to take the test again because they attended the earlier graduation. I was not going to let them down and especially not myself. It was difficult trying to survive at SIU because I had no car or job and dating women was impossible. Most of the girls wanted someone who worked at a job so you could wine and dine them, but during my senior year I managed to get a job as a dish washer at Walter Nit ties, but Andy the head chef fired me, but I missed working with the boys.

Early in the morning I received tutoring and took my test and had no problems with it. I knew the subject matter because there was someone in the writing lab who taught me much better and when I took the test I finished first. I checked with Mr. Ware and he said I completed the test and passed it but he still gave me a D after all that hard studying. Earlier Mr. Ware said, "You came here in 1971 and are leaving in 1973. That's unusual."

I went to University of Missouri, St. Louis, and took Advanced Composition, and received a B and a D in Problems in Teaching Reading and I could not understand how she taught this class. I realized much success came when I took Advanced Composition, and my English teacher said, "Charles your writing improved as I read each of your compositions."

My instructor made me write many papers coving different topics.

She said to me, "Charles why don't you take classes in journalism. You will get more writing courses then you would in an English program". By taking those two courses, it completed my 30 hours in English.

I remembered doing a project in Dr. Ware's class on black dialect showing how black kids did not speak standard English at home and left out the verbs when making a sentence.

I completed coursework in my teaching areas of social studies and English. Before that, I did my student teaching at East St. Louis Senior High School. Rudy Wilson, who was my African American university student teacher advisor, wanted me to dress professional but the only problem was I had not worked on a job for two years and did not have the money to buy suits and dress shoes. On one of his visits Rudy criticized me in front of the students and the principal called Rudy's dean and said they did not approve of this method of teaching. Later I explained to Rudy I was having a hard time trying to finish college with no money for expenses. Years later, when I was teaching professionally, I saw him in the cafeteria and he said," Hello Charles. You are dressing much better."

I told him about my experiences in the real world of professional teaching when I got a professional assignment at Cleveland High School, and wore suits all the time. As I matured, I could see what Rudy tried to teach me, but at the time I was twenty one, and did not see what he was talking about until at the age of twenty six when I was placed on probation, received tenure, and after three years; I saw dressing professional was very important. I graduated from Southern Illinois University at Edwardsville on June 18, 1974.

After graduation from SIUE in December of 1974, I traveled to the St. Louis Board Of Education and filled out an application to substitute teach. George Picket, the director of personnel talked to new perspective teachers.

"Charles it's just so many certified teachers and not enough positions but you have to start at the bottom first. "Mr. Picket said to me.

I stayed at home with my mother and step father Willie Winfield who retired from the United States government as an electrician helper. I was eager to work and make those five years of college pay off. One of my first teaching jobs was at a grade school located outside of Car Square Village on the city's North side of St, Louis in the downtown area. Ulla Flowers was the principal and she was strict when it came to student discipline.

I taught the fifth grade even though I was certified in secondary education. The thing about teaching elementary school was you taught at least 10 subjects during the day and graded many papers. I taught the students from April to June and passed all of them.

I met my second wife Vinita Washington while I was in graduate school. I happen to be doing some shopping and saw her and thought she was an attractive young woman. I told her I was in the graduate school working on my Master of Science degree in Counseling Education. I started in September of 1974 and graduated in June of

1975. My scholarship extended towards completing graduate work. I took two courses a quarter. In order to stay in the graduate program a student had to make a B or A to not get expelled. I took a course called Teaching Disadvantage Children, and I learned how to recognize and respect the culture of people growing up in low economic income families. The course called Humanistic Psychology was interesting and the instructor taught us about Maslow's hierarchy of needs and what was considered the most important aspects of your life. To learn how to teach people about careers and occupations, I took a course that taught the subject matter. Our instructor took us to different places of business to see how they operated. A major problem developed in my statistics class because I kept asking Dr. King about the math he was teaching. His method was to teach you but do not ask him any questions. One time he shouted at me in front of all the students which upset me very much. I went to another room during the break and tears of anger fell from my eyes. I should have filed a complaint against him but I thought about it and decided he was not going to make me drop this class and went back to hear his lecture, and did not ask him any more questions. I had come too far to be discouraged by the professor. I remembered when a white professor got angry at you and if you were black ; you would be earmarked for a low grade regardless of what type of great effort you put into passing the course. Most of the projects we turned in were group assignments and if I got a C the other students should have received a C also. I felt it was an unfair grade and I spoke to Howard and he said, "Charles do not let it get you down. Just keep on working." Howard told me he experienced the same problems as I did.

Venita and I saw each other at that time and tried to get a better understanding of each other but by the end of my graduation we were broken up. She wanted to get married but I had other plans. I was twenty five and not really mature for marriage. During that time, I lived on Washington Avenue in a big three story house. Kenneth Mitchell's mother owned the house and the students he went to school with called him Mitch. His height was 5' 10" and he was light skinned. Years later he shaved all his hair off.

Since I taught school as a substitute teacher Ken said I might want to get an apartment and he said, "Charles you should try to get a place to stay and you need your own apartment,"

I thought about it and moved into the apartment house owned by Ken's mother. The apartment consisted of a bedroom and kitchen. I enjoyed staying there and a fellow lived upstairs I communicated with asked me many things about my college career at SIU. He was light skinned and he possessed a great sense of humor. He wore a large Afro and played music on his stereo. Ken majored in acting and told me about the fun he enjoyed doing it.

From 1974 to 1975, I worked as a permanent substitute teacher at Soldan High School and for the first three months I taught English and social studies. I taught Shakespeare at first but the kids did not like the subject matter too much and neither did I. The students wanted to study something they could relate to. When Mr. Scot was absent because of illness, I taught his social studies classes for four months. There was one student who challenged me a lot and his name was Keith Mason. I helped him with his papers and he debated me most of the time, and I saw a smart student who would one day make something of himself. Another person I met at Soldan High School was Daniel Morris, he was also a substitute, and he taught in the area of physical education. Dan kept breaking his leg teaching classes and got workman's compensation for it. He became a great friend of mine and every Friday we got together and rode in Calvin's big black Mark 5, and went out to the park with a box of chicken, and kicked it up and unwound from five days of trying to teach the students. Calvin's band played at the Black Stark Club located on Lindell. Dan and Calvin were good friends of mine. Dan spent time in the Navy and graduated from Harris Stowe University with his degree in elementary education and later earned his Master's degree in special education from Webster University. During that year Dan dated Venita's sister Betty. I married Venita in 1984 and we had two children together, Benica in 1984, and Kalah in 1985. From 1974 to 1975, Venita and I courted each other, and most of the places we traveled to was by bus or cabs. The first date we went on was to a place called La Cassa, and we went to listen to a singing group called the Master's Touch. When Venita worked on some of her jobs, I took care of her son when I was staying with my mother. Sometimes we socialized at my mother's house when she was gone, but she never knew anything about it. Venita and I listened to music by Barry White. The first time Venita and I went out we took her son Dennis with us. Venita's family tree consisted of Marilyn, Betty, Marsha, Glen, and John Junior, who was named after his father John Washington Senior.

One humorous incident took place when Venita took me upstairs to her father's favorite third floor penthouse, an apartment complete with all the fittings a bachelor could want. I spent the night at the house and needed some clothes to sleep in and she gave me her father's pajamas. Venita's father came home and saw me in his night clothes and reclining in his bed upstairs. Later her father asked why did she let me wear his clothes and she said," Those clothes have been laying around up here and you never wear them. Charles needed something to sleep in so I told him he could wear your night garments." Being a minister her father, who was called Papa John, did not get too mad about the situation.

Sometimes Venita tried to get bad with me and one day I executed three or four hip throws on her but I kept her from hitting the sidewalk and I did not put a lot of force in the throws to keep her from getting hurt. Marriage did not fit into my plans at the time, and she wanted to do that, but I was not mature about it at the time when we dated each other from 1974 to 1975.

When I did not marry her, she left me which I later regretted. I remembered when her brother Glen cooked Thanks Giving dinner and invited his family and friends over to eat, He did not have much furniture for us to sit at or a table but no one said anything about it and we enjoyed the fact that he was humble and it did not bother us to be standing up eating. Glen probably just got settled in his apartment and did not have the money to furnish it with furniture at the time he invited friends over to eat for the holidays.

Glen played music by ear and when his father got married; he played music with members of his band at the reception. Venita and I enjoyed Bobby Humphrey who performed with the flute and Curtis Mayfield whose album "Super Fly" became a favorite of ours. Sometimes Venita came over to see me. Howard gave many house parties at his apartment and Venita and I attended them.

During the summer of 1975, I met Bertha Little at the employment office, and later we dated. In the courtship, I always came over to her brother's house and watched the football games. Bertha and I got married and our son Charles Pointer Junior was born in July of 1976. Bertha and I lived at my apartment until we put our money together and bought a two story house on Davison Avenue on the city's North side. Bertha's brother's name was Cleveland and his wife's name was Lynn and they liked playing cards. I helped raise my son from 1976 to 1981 and we purchased a house on Count Drive located in North St. Louis County,

Once I matured at the age of 54, I realized parents should attempt to keep their families together especially if they have kids, because it is difficult on them when divorces take place. The kids grow up with emotional scars hurting inside hating the absent parents because he or she is not playing a parental role in their lives. Sometimes the absent parents are blamed for the reasons a child ends up in prison or gets involved with the wrong influences that turn them into a life of drugs or crime living in the low income neighborhoods.

For my last requirements for my Master of Science degree in Counseling Education, I chose professors to serve on my committee and the sponsor was the third one. The professors asked me several questions about the courses I took and they approved my standing to get my Master of Science degree. I graduated on June 17, 1975 and my mother, brother, and grandmother attended the ceremony, and they were proud of me.

CHAPTER 5

1976 to Marriage Life and Teaching School

When I bought my 1977 Lincoln, Bertha, Charles Junior, and I enjoyed ourselves in the car and I visited many places in St. Louis, Missouri and St. Louis County. Bertha's brother Cleveland Little lived near us in another subdivision in a nice looking house and sometimes we visited him and his wife and played cards. I remember one summer we traveled to Cuba, Mississippi to see Bertha's mother and father. Cleveland's' wife Lynn went with us too. Bertha brother's name was Mason and I went out with him so he could show me around Cuba and Meridian, Mississippi, and as Mason drove down the road a driver in another car followed us.

"Don't worry! "Mason said. "I have a couple of shots left in my gun." Mason carried a gun with him but the people in the car did not know about it. Mason's height was about 6'1". Mason stopped the car and we jumped out and ran into a field and a house was located near it. We thought someone was following us but Mason knew them. We looked from behind the house as Mason spoke to his friends who got back into their cars and when we saw everything was alright we came from around the building.

I enjoyed looking at the countryside of Mississippi as Cleveland drove through the state, and I remembered the pine trees which lined the highway as we passed by them.

At an early age, Charles Junior attended nursery school, and his teacher was Mrs. Catherine, and she taught him early childhood education. I made sure he knew about our black cultural history such as there were black cowboys who helped tame the old west also.

I taught at the portables located on the east side of Beaumont High School in the spring of 1976 under the principal ship of Roman Poole teaching social studies before being sent to Cleveland High School where I taught social studies for four years.

During the summer of 1976, I checked in different parts of city government, and asked how I could get into working for a politician, and they told me Senator Raymond Howard looked for people to help him get votes. I immediately called Senator Howard who was African American and a lawyer.

Senator Howard said to me, "Charles I want you to get a team of workers together and win that ward for me. This ward is considered one of Senator Bank's strongest supporters, but can you defeat him?"

I said," I can do it but I need a job sir. My wife is having a baby and we'll need all the money we can get."

He said," That will not be a problem. I'll get you a job in the sheriff's office pasting mug shots of criminals in their files."

In the evening me and three or four workers canvassed the six or seven blocks and spoke to the neighbors about Senator Raymond

Howard and his friends called him Ray. His opponent Jet Banks served in the Missouri House of Representatives at the time and he attempted to be elected a state senator from the state of Missouri for the first time, and possessed a powerful organization working for him. Before the election, Senator Howard held a rally at his campaign headquarters and he inspired us to work hard to get voters to support him on the day of the election.

Before the election, Senator Howard came and walked with us to the different houses and spoke with the neighbors and one of the first things he asked us was if the people knew about him or if we placed campaign literature in their mailboxes about him and in many instances we said yes.

On the day of the election there was much activity and a heavy voter turnout. It was fun working with the people who canvassed the neighborhood with me trying to get the votes for Senator Raymond Howard. We lost the election, but I won my ward by a couple votes. The people we spoke to remembered us when they came to vote.

The house on Davison was located down the street from Walbridge Elementary and by that time in 1976 most of the white residents moved out of the North Side. Next door to us lived an elderly white couple and we became good friends of theirs. They probably were in their 70's or 80's at that time. Across the street was a family of black people who received a lot of friends coming in and out of their house. When I left to teach at Cleveland High School, they sat on their porch watching me come in every evening. Sometimes I walked through the alley so my neighbors across the street would not know my schedule. Burglars constantly broke into the houses on Davison Avenue and many of the residents placed steel bars on their windows and doors. I got a dog and put him in the back yard and he kept up a lot of noise most of the time.

My wife Bertha helped me buy furniture and we shared the same responsibilities. Most of her duties consisted of talking care of my son while I worked as a teacher. I paid the bills and did many things around the house like cutting the grass, painting the house, and anything that kept the house whole functioning.

The summer of 1976 came to an end, and I prepared to go back to school to work for the St. Louis Board of Education. Before the summer of 1976, I worked at Beaumont High School as a social studies teacher and Mr. Roman Pool was the principal.

The principal of Cleveland High School looked for a social studies teacher to come in as a permanent sub and complete the school year. They held interviews for the position, and I went to Cleveland High School and applied for the job.

When I arrived Mr. Nimo and Dr. Albert Reinsch sat at a table and I gave them my resume which showed my Associate of Arts degree in Liberal Arts, a Bachelor of Science degree in Secondary Education with a major in history and a minor in English.

Dr. Reinsch said, "Mr. Nimo in reviewing Mr. Pointer's resume he is what we are looking for regardless to if you knew him or not. Mr.Pointer you are qualified for this position."

"Charles it's nice seeing you again." Mr. Nimo said.

Mr. Nimo, an African American, was an assistant principal at O'Fallon Technical High School when I attended that high school from 1964 to 1968. When traveling to the south side of St. Louis, I had never been to that side of town before and it was predominantly Caucasian.

Sometimes I got lost coming from that area because I was not from the neighborhood.

At that school, I experienced many things and got interested in people both black and white. I taught social studies at Cleveland High School.

Teaching some of the students was troubling because one student who was having discipline problems said I taught too much black history?

Dr. Reinsch said, "The only thing Mr. Pointer did was showed where black people were left out of the history books."

Teaching at Cleveland High reflected back on a time from 1961 to 1963 when I was bussed to Walbridge Elementary as a student and how our group was placed in separate lunch facilities, recess, and all the black student classes did not have white students in them.

Now I was taking part in history to be one of the first groups of black teachers being sent to Cleveland High School before black students were to take part in desegregation efforts ordered by the courts. All of the students in my classes were white at first. I met Donald Bright, who was African American, and he became a good friend of mine and served as a good role model for me. Donald came from Dallas, Texas. At the time I met Donald he came to Cleveland High School to teach mathematics as a permanent substitute teacher. Later Donald went to Webster University and earned his Master of Science degree in Mathematics and he became a great innovator in teaching that subject matter. Through the years Donald gave helpful advice on most anything I wanted to talk about which became helpful to me. The St. Louis Public School System became the first organization to let Donald Bright teach students mathematics through the use of television. Donald advised me one evening when a teacher came into my classroom and criticized me in front of the students and he said, "Charlie you did the best thing to write the principal to explain what he did instead of having a racial debate with the students looking at it. With the principal talking to him about it, he will not do it again. It's a good thing the teacher came and apologized to you about it."

Donald's love for music excited me about a song he always played and singed called "A One in A Million You "by George Clinton. Being appreciative about the song Donald said, "That song is beautiful Charley. It makes me feel very good inside every time I play it."

When talking with Donald, I learned he was married and had two children. His son's name was Donny who he named after a preacher who pastured at a church in Dallas, Texas. Donald was in a car accident when a driver ran a stop light and hit the side of his door which resulted in him getting five broken ribs. Five years after that, Donald resigned from the Riverview Gardens School District as a math teacher. His wife

Mary Ann said Donald went home to spend time with his family in Dallas where he died.

The school board in St. Louis, MO laid off teachers whom they felt did not have their certification. I told Donald, I attended the University of Missouri, St. Louis and took courses called Exceptional Children, Advanced Composition, and Problems in Teaching Reading and the state of Missouri awarded me English certification grades 7 through 12.

Donald said," Charlie you might have the certification already so why don't you check things out to see if you do."

I did what Donald told me and the school board called me back to work.

With his passing, I really missed him because he acted like a big brother to me, and showed much kindness, and love when I needed a friend to depend on. I will always miss the times when I got a chance to talk with him about the experiences in life which interested me, and Donald gave me advice and counseled me on many things especially when I went through two divorces.

With the need to get rid of some his clothes, Donald gave me many named brands of shoes, shirts, slacks, and some suits. Knowing about his vast amount of knowledge in accounting, Donald tutored me in that subject matter and I passed the course.

Going to Moore's Barber shop brought many memorable times because Donald, and I went there to get our hair cut, and we talked about many topics with other customers on civic events taking place in the community. Sports became a good topic for discussion. We mostly talked about the NFL team, the Dallas Cowboys because Donald was from that city and he loved the football team.

I became frustrated during the years attempting to get into thirty law schools and faced rejection from each of them after paying over $1200 dollars in application fees. I worked two jobs to pay the cost of applying to those law schools

As I spoke to Donald, he said, "Charles you're going to have to attempt many other things to become successful and just do not concentrate on law school. It will make you miserable."

Taking Donald's advice, I went to criminal justice school at the University of Missouri, St. Louis and earned a Bachelor of Science degree in 2001 in Criminal Justice and made the Dean's List and four years later earned my Associate of Arts degree in Paralegal Studies which made me want to attend a law school much later in life. I remembered the times when Donald improved his certification in math by attending Webster University and he earned a Master of Science degree in that subject matter. Donald said to me, "Charles the problems I worked on can cover a lot of space. Sometimes learning math was very exhausting." His first certification was in social studies but it tended to be over crowed prompting him to get certified in mathematics to start a new subject area teaching career. As a math teacher, Donald taught in the Upwards Bound Program at St. Louis University and commented about a professor and he said, "Charles there's a faculty member who never irons his shirt before he comes to work. Just because he has a PHD does not mean he should ignore the way he wears his shirts."

As a college student, Donald played fullback on the football team and served as a second lieutenant in the army and attended Bishop College.

When speaking with Donald, he told me his father said to him before he died, "Do not ever chase after a woman who does not love you."

I learned many important things about life which Donald taught me in our 34 year relationship, because I learned how to be humble and use intelligent methods to handle my personal problems.

Donald said to me," Stop calling someone who does not love you even if it's the women you married, because it will not benefit you whatsoever. Concentrate on women, who care and love you; you will feel much better about yourself if you do this in your relationships with women."

Donald always stressed keeping a good appearance and especially keeping your shoes shinned, and a neat haircut when applying for jobs and wearing suits to a job interview. When I first met Donald at Cleveland High School, his sense of humor touched me very deeply, and I enjoyed talking with him. For a while he needed a ride to the dentist so I said to him, "I'll take you to the dentist so you can make your appointment." Later on Donald bought a green colored Plymouth automobile. The teachers went on strike, and Donald chose not to join it, because he was attempting to get a teaching position with the school board, and felt he could not afford to make the school board officials angry stopping him from getting hired as a probationary teacher in the math department. Even though I joined the strike our friendship did not stop when it was over.

Another person who became a friend of mine taught art and I called him Cullen and his last name was Cook. While attending college, Cullen played in the band on a music scholarship, and his passion became singing karaoke, and currently Cullen sings songs, and they are played on u-tube. His voice is beautiful as he sings those songs like the big stars.

As he got older, I kept telling Cullen to give up teaching, and start a singing career and art is an interesting subject Cullen deals with because he can paint pretty oil paintings. In Cullen's basement, there are many paintings of oil pictures done by him. Another ambition of Cullen's resulted in him volunteering to learn school administration at Cleveland High School. Cullen went back to college and got certified as a school principal, and with much hard work became a principal at the Juvenile Center for many years until he retired. When I needed a recommendation for a job, he wrote one for me. Sometimes when Cullen's car needed repairs; he rode to Cleveland High with me in the morning.

Louise Mitchell, an African American, taught for the St. Louis Public School System for at least twenty years, and her specialty was special education. Her son Filex was my student when I taught at Beaumont High School, before I was assigned to Cleveland High School. Her husband, whom she called Peaches, was an engineer, and she always spoke well about him. Before I got my car, Mrs. Mitchell drove down Grand Boulevard, and dropped me off at a bus stop, so I could catch the next bus to take me home. When I needed help in my teaching assignments, she gave me advice on how to become a good teacher and person. Being a good mother, Mrs. Mitchell loved her husband. Felix went into the mortuary science field and his sister Jeanie taught school. Even though deceased, I will never forget her, and the love she showed me as a beginning teacher. When visiting Mrs. Mitchel's classes, much activity took place as she taught her students.

Another fellow teacher I met at Cleveland High School was an African American by the name of James Williams, and he taught social studies. Jim lived a few blocks away from me on a street called Prince Avenue. Jim's height was about 5'5", and he weighed about 150 pounds, and sported a mustache. Every evening we rode home together, and Jim worked as a paramedic on an ambulance at night, and taught school in the morning. I could not believe how he did it but it did not seem to bother him even though Jim was married and had a daughter. I met a friend of Jim's at his house and I later wrote a 24 page document about Charles Robert Henry who served a tour of duty in Vietnam during the war.

As the years progressed at Cleveland High School from 1976 to 1980, the school administration placed me on probation and after three months I was evaluated. The room was quiet when Dr. Albert Reinsch came into my room and watched me teach my students. With my lesson plans prepared, the students and I participated in class discussions about topics we studied in United States history.

I showed films on different periods of history. One amazing discovery I witnessed when traveling to Cleveland High School was seeing a part of St. Louis, I did not know anything about. Sometimes I did not take the highway home and drove through different neighborhood sites on the Southside of St. Louis, MO to compare our neighborhood with theirs. Cleveland High School was mostly populated with white students. Curiosity filled their eyes when they asked me what it was like to attend a black high school.

I said, "I cannot be the spokesperson for the black population on this issue. You are going to have to attend a school with a lot of black students and see for yourself what it's like to be associated with them."

When I really wanted my students to learn, I worked hard with them. Many of my students did not know anything about writing a thesis, and I decided to teach them how to write term papers the way Dr. Rosenfeld taught me.

Every day I brought notes, and wrote what I wanted them to know on the black board. Sometimes I heard boos coming from students when I came into the classroom.

I was able to undergo the pressures of teaching all white students because in most of my college classes at SIU, I was the only black student. A group of students were in the hallway talking with each other, and as I passed by I heard one of them shout, "Hey Buck Wheat!" and laughed.

Instead of going to them and asking why they were treating me this way; I went to the nicest administrator, who felt much concern for teachers, who experienced problems adjusting to deal with racial problems among staff, and students. His name was Max Carlisle.

I said to Mr. Carlisle," A group of students are calling me Buckwheat. Could you try to find out who was responsible for this?"

By speaking with various students, he located the students and disciplined them.

News quickly spread Cleveland High School would be integrated by black students and thoughts about it might become a reality. The challenge of school integration took charge and the students participated in demonstrations in front of the school, because rumors circulated white students were being transferred to schools on the North side, where the majority of the students were black.

At first everything was ok and then problems started. The black students felt Dr. Reinch ignored their concerns. Teachers noticed unusual things about the black students which were negative. It appeared these students were not motivated about getting a good education. Information circulated around the staff and counselors at Soldan High School that they sent Cleveland High School their worst slow learning students, and Cleveland High School sent them their smartest ones. Tensions grew and a riot broke out at Cleveland High School. Jim and I helped break up fights between the black and white students. Students fought on the lawns and eventually the police arrived and broke up the fighting. I never thought I would be in the middle of a race riot to witness black and white students fighting each other.

Many of the black faculty left out of the back door of the school instead of going to the front of the building where the students protested a few days before the riot started. I left out the front of Cleveland High School regardless of if I might get insulted, or hurt as I walked through the crowd. I heard shouting and protesting, and I saw some of my students expressing their first amendment rights of freedom of speech.

Regardless to what took place, the teachers and administrators were determined to make integration work at Cleveland High School and later its name was changed to Cleveland ROTC High School. Many of my students asked what was it like in the black schools and after they experienced it ;one of them by the name of Bissell said to me, "Mr. Pointer it's nice being educated with black students, plus I joined the soccer team."

CHAPTER 6

DR. HOWARD JUNIOR MILLER'S ELECTION FOR STATE REPRESENTATIVE OF MISSOURI

While I was a teacher at Cleveland High School from 1976 to 1980, Howard taught social work courses at Southern Illinois University at Edwardsville and a major goal he shared with me was he wanted to run for the office of state representative of Missouri.

One day when Howard and I were in the paper room in the Commercial Art Department at O'Fallon Technical High School Howard said to me, "Charles I am going to run for public office one day."

Being probably 15 or 16 years old at the time, I knew he was serious and years later he completed his Bachelor of Science degree in Sociology at the University of Missouri, St. Louis, Missouri and his Master of Social Work at Washington University, St. Louis, MO and did several years of teaching at many universities. Howard wanted to enter the political arena and took his old high school buddy into this adventure with him, which was something that would be long remembered many years later when he received his PHD in higher education.

To begin his campaign for state representative, Howard started months in advance to get his agenda together, to tell the voters what he wanted to do, to make their community a better place to live in.

Flyers were printed out and Howard passed them out to people on the streets of St. Louis as people drove by in their cars. To get ready, he set up his headquarters. Howard rented a business store front on Union but later closed it down and joined forces with Vervus Jones who ran for committeeman and Laverne Olive who ran for committeewoman, and their headquarters were located at Lillian and Davison on the city's North side. To raise money, Howard and his wife Ruth Ann Miller organized a fashion show, which was a nice strategy to bring city officials and residents to see black people could organize their own resources, to do something like this. Clothing stores did not mind having their fashions displayed in hopes of creating future sales for them. The models looked nice as they strolled down the walkway and stood in front of the audience who admired the clothes they displayed.

Better ideas were generated by Howard's organization by talking to voters in the district he was running for state representative, in the city of St. Louis, MO. Some people who supported the Miller, Jones, and Olive ticket took part in the parade as we rode through the city. I was in the parade too. People standing on the sidewalks waved and made us happy to see many of them receptive to our intentions. One thing which impressed me about Howard was the energy he possessed, to take on those responsibilities, and be a family man at the same time. This was during the summer months and we canvassed most of the evening and during the day. Howard wanted to keep on campaigning into the next morning. After a few heated debates I decided to go home and get some rest. Years later, I understood where Howard was coming from when I did prose work in court and when my first book published by Xlibris called 'The Making of a Black Belt Karate Champion", took much hard work to accomplish this, and when I did 23 pro-se cases in the 8th Circuit Federal Court, and about 13 in the appellate court, and oral argument in the 22th Missouri Appellate Court Of Appeals. In the political race working with Howard, he influenced me to put 100 % into everything I did and more.

On election day everyone prepared to get our candidate elected and much excitement circulated through our campaign headquarters. At the last minute Howard approached me and said, "Charles we did not get funds to make a mailing to let voters in our ward know what our agenda to improving the quality of life in their community was all about. I lent Howard $ 700 dollars to make a mailing to the voters in our ward to get the message out about improvements we wanted to make in the community. When the end of the day came, we lost the election.

Much cheating took place and we concluded how could a white person win an election in a ward that was 99% black. Someone placed our candidate on ballots in the wrong ward which I brought to Howard's attention.

CHAPTER 7

COUNT DRIVE 1976 TO 1980

The neighborhood on Davison in the Walnut Park area developed into a community of high rising crime and criminals broke into many houses located on our block so my wife and I decided to buy a house in North County located on Count Drive. I paid $2,000 dollars down and got a loan to finance the rest. The house consisted of a living room, two bed rooms, a kitchen, a large basement, and big backyard. My son Charles Junior was two years old at the time. The living room, hallway and kitchen floor were carpeted.

My neighbor Clyde Day was Caucasian and he became a good friend of mine. A lot of evenings we talked with each other about many things and Clyde had several kids, and he and his wife worked hard to raise them, and kept good family ties with each other. Clyde taught me a lot of things about keeping a house in good repair. I mowed the lawn and planted trees in front of the house. The trees grew large as the years progressed. Some of our white neighbors' kids cursed at you when driving down the street because they resented black people moving into the neighborhood. Other white families lived around us and across the street but they were friendly. The subdivision we lived in was called Castle Point. Eventually Bertha got a job in a government program which was a great help to pay some bills. My summers were

left because her brother kept on asking for money and I grew tired of him doing this. I went home for a while but came back to Sharon but she moved to another residence so I did not know where she was but 30 years later my daughter and I met each other and Sharon and I renewed our friendship again. I moved to an apartment complex after I could not find Sharon located on Lucus and Hunt and highway 70. The apartment complex I moved to was nice. There was a lady who lived in an apartment who came out to walk her dog and I spent much time getting to know her. This was 1982 and it snowed so heavily it was difficult getting to the grocery store. I still taught in the school system and earned enough to pay the rent, and buy a living room set, and a bed to sleep in. I stayed at the apartment complex for a little while, but went back home to 10504 Count Drive because I did not have employment teaching school for the summer. My relationship with Bertha deteriorated and I went to live with my mother and she tried to tell me not to live with other women too quickly but I moved in with Venita who resided on Cates Avenue. I was transferred to Northwest High School in 1980 and stayed there for a year. English was my minor and I taught in a Title One program. It took too long for us to get our books and the classes consisted of at least six students. One of the most interesting events which happened to me at Northwest High School influenced me to get my Bachelor of Science degree in Journalism was when I wrote an essay on "The Interpretation of Dr. Martin Luther King's Speech called I Have a Dream." I read his speech and gave my own meaning of what he said in his speech. George Curby, who worked for the St. Louis American News Paper, published it in his newspaper. Many people enjoyed reading it and thousands of people got the newspaper and read my essay. This essay was placed in the newspapers and viewed by thousands of St. Louis citizens.

When my book the" Making of a Black Belt Karate Champion" was published on March 20, 2012 Cullen said, "Charles you started out as a local writer and now you are an international one." That book is selling all over the world in countries like England, Italy, Australia, Japan, and Germany to name a few of them and the United States.

In 1981, I decided to date Venita while I was with Bertha whom I just could not get alone with. I called her and said I would like to take her out to dinner. Venita lived on the corner of Cates and Hamilton. Miss. Pritchard was the landlady and she talked like a lady of prominence. There were many reasons for living with Venita but the bottom line was I was just trying to be happy. Venita wanted to be in control of the relationship and I did not realize what problems I would encounter developing a relationship with her. Sometimes women will be with a person for love and in many cases it would be for money. When I worked as a teacher making decent money, Venita treated me good, but when I was forced to resign from my teaching job the kind treatment ended.

CHAPTER 8

MY TEACHING CAREER AT VASHON HIGH SCHOOL FROM 1981 TO 1984

Vashon High School was located on Bell Avenue but the side of the building faced Grand Avenue where a lot of traffic traveled on it. The school parking lot was located on that side and a football field was in that area too. Before the start of the school year, I went to the University of Missouri at St. Louis and took Advanced Composition and a course called Problems in Teaching Reading and fulfilled my

English certification grades 7-12. The school board sent letters to certain teachers saying they were not fully certified and I was one of them. I told school officials I had my certification before school started, and I showed them my teacher's license and I received a call from a board member to report to Vashon High School. I taught a subject called Essential Skills of English, but I missed the training the other teachers received to teach this new area of English the students were learning. I taught grades 9 through 12 and my freshmen classes were the noisiest but I kept my students working. Every time a school administrator came in he gave me a bad evaluation and I told them I was not trained in that subject matter like the other teachers. Regardless of how I tried to teach the subject matter; I felt a conspiracy developing to get me fired. I went to the principal Mr. Williams and asked for a transfer, but he refused my request. During the strike, I took part in it and I did not regret my actions because of the two years of mistreatment given to me by the principal Mr. Williams, and the school administrators. I was escorted out of the school by two security officials and suspended pending a hearing which never came.

I resigned which was not the best thing to do and years later when I studied employment law, I realized I was not advised of the problems associated with resigning. When you do that, you give up your rights to bring charges against employers, who discharge you unfairly. The only thing I thought about was taking care of my family, and by resigning I could use the $ 5,000 dollars pension money saved from my retirement fund, after being placed on probation and earning tenure after three years of teaching.

The union representative did not advise me properly about the hazards of resigning. I could not get a teaching job in another school district with a suspension pending a hearing on my employment record. At that time we stayed at Countryside Apartments and in 1984 my daughter Benica Jane Pointer was born. I'll never forget the night my daughter Benica was born when Venita's water broke and she screamed and shouted at me to take her to the hospital. Howard and his wife left an hour earlier. I never saw a woman giving birth before and this was an exciting experience for me, being in the operating room seeing Benica being born in August of 1984 and earlier that year;

I received my specialized certificate in journalism from Washington University, St. Louis, Missouri.

I managed to get a job at the Stake and Shake Restaurant at night and took care of Benica during the day and went to Washington University at night taking my journalism courses. Venita's son Dennis was no more than 14 or 15 years old at the time, he lived with us. When he turned eighteen, he served in the first Persian Gulf War, driving a truck. As a youngster, he attended Catholic schools and one of them was called Little Flower. After serving in the Persian Gulf, Dennis became a successful life insurance salesman.

Venita's father's name was John Washington, Sr. She had three sisters by the names of Betty, Marilyn, and Marsha and two Brothers, John Jr. and Glen. Glen's passion was music and he played in a band. Betty went to school and possessed several certificates in different careers. The family lived in a big three story house located on Wabada Avenue. Their father, who they called Pa Pa John, was a former pastor of his own church and resided over his own store which he sold reused goods and the second floor contained many rooms. His sister stayed in one of them.

In 1985, Kalah Pointer was born in August after I graduated from Washington University, St. Louis, MO during the month of June with a Bachelor of Science degree in Journalism. Since it was difficult finding a job, we moved to Venita's father's house located over his store. Next, we moved to Shaw Avenue and rented an apartment and Venita got employed at Learner's Clothing Store which sold women's clothes. I could not get a job in teaching because of bad recommendations, but I still did not give up trying, and wrote for the local newspapers as a freelance writer.

CHAPTER 9

1985 TO 1990 TRYING TO OVER COME ADVERSITY AND MOVE ON TO SUCCESS

I worked for the Bellefontaine Rehabilitation Center in 1987 as a QMRP, and my clients were brain dead, and lived in cottages. We tried to teach them social skills.

Trying to get other employment, I worked for Labor World and Ozzies going to temporary jobs assignments, and I worked at a marketing company called Marketeam doing surveys. In the area of cleaning, I worked at Hoch Junior High during the evenings, and was falsely accused of going into a girl's restroom, and fired on hearsay evidence. I found out the supervisor who fired me had a lot of relatives who were out of work and did some foul play to make me lose my job. They did not have a hearing to hear my side of the story. I saw the supervisor in the Goodwill Store and spoke to her friend Jesse and that same female supervisor who accused me of doing this walked away quickly without saying anything to me.

At that time I worked at Stake and Shake and if you stayed long enough you ended up learning how to cook, clean, and wait on customers. When I met Eddie, he and I became good friends. Eddie married Betty, a Caucasian. I earned tips waiting on customers, and used the money to buy food. Regardless of the type of job I worked on,

I did it because my kids needed to be taken care of. Shaw Avenue was located on the South Side of St. Louis, Missouri, and Shaw's Garden was up the street from where I lived. Shaw's Garden contained thousands of plants and people came from many parts of the world to see them.

When I took biology at O'Fallon Technical High School under Mr. White's supervision in 1964, I traveled to Shaw's Garden and collected leaves for an assignment he gave us to do.

I caught the bus and went to work at Stake and Shake and attended Washington University much earlier in the evening from 5.p.m. to 7.p.m. When my first ex-wife Bertha got the child support organization to garnish my check my married life became a nightmare. While I worked at Stake and Shake, a sheriff deputy came to the restaurant and gave me a document instructing me not to come back home. Every time I came home after working from 11 p.m. to 7a.m, Venita called the police, and they took me to jail. This happened many times until I realized it was best for me to go to my mother's house to stay. It was hard on me not being at home with my daughters who were one and two years old at the time. My mother brought me over to the house one evening to get some things and my daughters cried when I was leaving;I could not do anything but cry inside, not knowing I would only see my kids once from 1987 to 2003. I tried to stay in touch but it was difficult doing this. My mother kept criticizing me because she felt I shouldn't have kept staying in the back room of her apartment sitting in a rocking chair thinking about the situation.

"She said," Charles you cannot sit in that chair and feel bad about what happened. You have to get on with your life," I thought about what she said and decided to take her advice. With the type of education I had, I sent out resumes to different companies hoping to get job offers.

It was difficult getting a teaching job because of bad references but I never gave up. Eventually my mother and I were on bad terms because of the manner in which she spoke to me so I went to the Salvation Army located on Washington Avenue. Most of the men came to spend the night because their wives put them out, by getting restraining orders from the courts. The judges listened to the women without the man or father being there to hear their side of the story because men were not summoned to appear in court to defend themselves against the accusations. The men slept on a concrete floor and at that time they did not have shower facilities, and the smell made you sick. Every morning I got up and looked for work. The nearest place was Atlas and that's where I went to be sent out to different manual labor jobs. They sent me to a residence passed Highway 270 where a worker was putting tiles on a roof. This fellow did not talk to me with respect and positioned me on top of a roof with tiles coming up to the side of the roof where I took them off the conveyer belt. The conveyer belt sent the tiles up so quickly I could not get them off fast enough and he yelled at me. Realizing I did not like his attitude, I came down the ladder after he went up to the roof to collect the tiles. While he was on the roof, I left and went home. Strolling down the street, I could not wait to get on the bus which took me home. One time Atlas sent me to a place that packed cement bags. The machine packed the concrete materials into a bag and I placed the bag on a pallet. The supervisor who was Caucasian kept telling me to speed it up which I could not do and I told them I was going home. The other men told the supervisor I drove them out to the job site and they had to leave with me and if I left, the assignment would not be completed. The supervisor agreed to let me finish the assignment without doing any work. Not giving up hope in me, Atlas sent me to a company with a steady ticket where I washed dishes, and it was ok because I could get free meals. My drive on the highway to the company was ok too. I remembered when the company sent me to the county to knock down walls in a big building with a steel hammer.

Sometimes during the winter months, I found myself sleeping in my car outside in front of the Salvation Army and one night I heard a sound on the passenger side of the car, and it waked me up, and as I looked into the face of someone who was trying to break into my car I gave out a yell, and he yelled too because he did not know anyone was in the car. At once he ran down the street, and I pushed on the gas pedal and drove off real fast. I remember one night all of us were sleeping in our beds and every one of us told each other where we came from. One of the brothers asked a fellow from Africa where he was from and he said, "I am from London." All the brothers looked at him in a strange way and laughed and one of them said, "What are you doing in this place?" The brother felt that if he came from London he should not be in this place as if there were no ghettoes in England. One morning three of us slept in my car in the cold and one of the fellows said," Turn on the heat and I said, "It will burn my gas up and you can go if you do not like it in here." One thing I liked about staying at the Salvation Army was the religious teachings of God and they held bible classes for us to attend. In my attempts to get a job, two hundred miles away at a mental health institute, I drove my Cadillac and there was a hole in my gas tank, and it leaked. I had to leave my car at a gas station, for repairs. I told the man, I would come back and pay him, once I got back to work, to earn the money, to pay for repairs. Instead of going back to St. Louis, MO, I took my suit and shoes with me and marched down the highway to get to the interview. I met some interesting people who stopped and gave me rides like a truck driver who wanted to help me, and let me off on the side of the highway when he was going in a different direction. My feet kept hurting me as I walked towards the mental health facility, but looking at the countryside was beautiful. When walking over a bridge, I bent down low and held on to the metal bars to keep from being pulled into the highway from air pressure generated from the tires of the big 16 wheeler transfer trucks. The next fifty or so miles, I ran into three other people on the highway, who traveled in the same direction as I, and they were good company. At the end of my journey, a person driving a truck stopped and offered me a lift to the town I was traveling to. Feeling very tired, I made it to the mental health center limping, and they interviewed me, and bought a ticket for my return home. I did not get hired, but after earning the money when I came back home; I took a trip to the filling station, and paid the mechanic for fixing my car.

When I was at my mother's house, I remembered getting a magazine which told people how to make money, but I did not pay it much attention. One evening, I received a letter to come to Jefferson City, Missouri to interview for a job. Getting off the bus, I walked through Jefferson City near Lincoln University, and went to the nearest Salvation Army, and they let me spend the night. I woke up in the morning, and was surrounded by white folks. After getting dressed and eating, I went outside and saw a man cleaning his car windows.

"What are you doing? "I asked him. He said, "I am cleaning my car windows and this is how I make my money when I am on the road." I said, "How do you make money like that?"

"All you have to do is get some window squeezes, go to different businesses and ask to wash their windows," he said.

"You will be able to make some money if you work hard at it."

After the interview, I did not get the job. There were three or four people sitting at the table asking me a lot of questions but nothing else developed after that, but one thing I learned was how to make money cleaning windows, so I kept that in mind coming back from Jefferson City.

After leaving the Atlas Company without being sent out on a job, I thought about the gentleman at the Salvation Army, and what he told me about cleaning windows, and decided I would do the same thing.

The first windows I cleaned were a group of businesses on Natural Bridge Avenue, but I owned squeezes which cleaned car windows but I did not know any better. A long handle holding mop was used to clean the large windows and I wiped them with a squeeze making the window look sparkling clean. At first, I charged about 10 dollars a window. The only materials I used to clean the windows were ammonia and water. After doing the smaller windows, I wanted to work for larger businesses and I saw this big building called McGuire's Moving and Storage which had two stories of windows. I asked the proprietor Mr. McGuire if I could wash his windows and he said," It was ok. Just give me a price."

"I can do them for one hundred dollars," I said.

The deal was made and I washed the windows until the owner's son came and spoke to me.

"Charles I've seen what is used to clean windows and you are using a car window squeeze, "he said.

It never occurred to me I used the wrong cleaning tools.

I said, "There's a hardware store nearby. May I go across the street and buy one?"

Knowing I did not have any money, I went to the hardware store and spoke with the clerk and said to him, "I got this window cleaning job a cross the street. I do not have the right squeeze to finish the job. Could you let me borrow one of yours and I'll pay you back after I get finished with the windows."

The clerk thought about what I said and wondered would I bring the squeeze back and said," I trust you but come back and pay for it."

I rushed to Mr. McGuire's and finished his windows for one hundred dollars and paid the hard ware clerk his money and thanked Mr. McGuire and the clerk because he trusted an unknown stranger who was black and he was Caucasian and saw I was trying to earn some money the honest way, and needed someone to give me an opportunity to better my economic position. This fellow put his job on the line for me and I will never forget his kindness.

I'll never forget the kindness shown to me by Mr. McGuire and his son and Mr. McGuire told me when he got started; he use to sell coal to his neighbors and different goods to take care of his family, and I guess he saw himself in the same position many years ago when he first started his business with little or no money and became a success and gave me an opportunity to make money the honest way. Now he owns one of the largest moving and storage companies in St. Louis, MO, and he sold furniture at the time when I worked for him.

At first, I used my feet to get me where I wanted to go or caught the bus but I needed reliable transportation. Not too far from McGuire's was a fellow who sold used cars and I came into his office and said, "I would like to buy this LTD car."

"What type of work do you do?"

I said, "I have a window cleaning business."

I listed all of the places I cleaned windows at and he said, "Just give me about $ 100 dollars as a down payment and pay me $ 50 dollars every two weeks." After giving him the money, I was in business. With the help of God, I established constant business with Radio Shack, Nationals Food Store, and many businesses on Grand Avenue and throughout the city of St. Louis, Missouri. Trying to get business, I stopped at a retail shop where the business owner was a black lady and I spoke to her and asked if I could wash her windows and she said, "It will be ok Charles and why don't you asked the owner of this building could you wash his also." The owner said it was ok to wash his windows too. I cleaned her windows and she told me about her daughter who was in the service. To get business, I drove down the street and got out of my car and left the motor running and asked the business owners if they wanted their windows cleaned.

While doing the window cleaning, I met a black woman by the name of Nettie who owned the Original Restaurant and people from all parts of the city came to eat her soul food.

"May I clean your windows Mrs. Nettie?" and she said, "Sure" and told me what windows she wanted cleaned. Nettie treated me with respect and she said to me," How would you like to work here in the evenings after finishing cleaning windows all day? "Many gospel singers came to her restaurant to eat. I remember seeing Shirley Cesar eating one evening at the restaurant after a show. When I could not get into the Salvation Army at night, I slept in my car at night and looked at the stars and thought about my life, and how did I get myself into this situation. Sometimes I ventured on the south side of St. Louis and parked my car in the park only to have a policeman ask me to leave.

On the north side this never would happen in our neighborhood parks. When I got steady work from Atlas, I resided at a hotel containing rooms with one restroom in them. A fellow by the name of Herbert lived in one of the rooms and this brother was tall and wore a mustache and he drank a lot. The rent was fifty dollars a week which I was able to pay because I went to work every day to pay it with no problem. The employment company sent me to work in the county and as I traveled to work a police officer directed the traffic and I got in the wrong lane and turned instead of coming forward and he gave me a ticket. The police officer told me to follow him to the police station.

The police officer said, "Sir you are under arrest. Your wife has a warrant for your arrest for child support."

The police officer copied my fingerprints and transferred me to a prison located on Highway 40. This shocked me and I found myself in a cell with six fellows who were in jail for crimes related things and they took a survey of what they were in jail for and I heard different reasons from each of them. Most of the fellows said they were incarcerated for crimes such as stealing, burglary, auto theft, and when I said child support laughter broke out from all of them when they heard what I told them. I noticed one of my cellmates possessed fifty women photographs of his girlfriends, and he asked me if I could write one of them a letter which I did because I told them I was a former English teacher.

By the time I called my mother and told her what took place; Ronald spoke to my cousin Darleen Green, whose boyfriend was a lawyer. I met him when he came out to the prison to speak with me.

Jerome was my attorney's name and he said, "You do not have to explain anything to me because your brother told me what took place." He told them to transfer me to a dormitory with fellows who had minor offenses against them because I was put in a cell with people with felonies and child support was a misdemeanor, but I enjoyed the company of the fellows who had major crimes on their records. They treated me like family, and I will never forget the good times we talked about life in general.

My attorney explained everything to the judge saying the notice to appear in court went to my mother's address and when I appeared in court the judge said. "Good luck." When I obtained employment, I gave my mother money for paying my rent while I was in jail and when I got out; my attorney was paid five hundred dollars. My mother, brother, and Darlene played a role in getting me out of jail, and at the writing of this book I am very grateful for their help.

I went home and stayed with my mother and my stepfather, Willie Winfield, who knew someone that rented apartments at a big house located on Grand and Cook Avenue. The big three story house sat across from Saint Alphonso Catholic Church. When passing the church, its services appeared to be loud because hearing the clapping and shouting made it seemed like this was a Baptist Church. Usually Catholic Church services are quiet. Joe managed the apartment house and collected rent. His height was about 5'3" and he weighed about 160 pounds and he loved eating fruit. I stayed on the third floor and the kitchen provided a place for us to cook.

My friend Garry stayed in the next building, and I remembered many things about him and his height was about 5'4" and Garry smoked and drank a lot. On some summer nights, I went over to Garry's house and he played records by Motown Records recording artists and we singed the night away for fun. One hot summer day Garry, and I bought some beer got intoxicated and singed our favorite Motown hits. The address 1127 North Grand brought many memories to me when we formed lines waiting for a person to come out the restroom, or when we wanted to wash up to go to work in a hurry, and this became a constant problem, but we managed to work it out.

James lived in the room across from me and too much drinking became a majored problem for him, but he treated you with respect, and sometimes when I came home, his body was folded across the kitchen table, and he could not make it up the stairs, because he drank too much.

Robert stayed on the second floor, and he worked at the Stake House as a cook, and the restaurant was located across the street, in front of the Fox Theater, where many big time stars in the entertainment world gave concerts.

One thing I learned from Garry was he taught me how to go hustling with him to do things to make money, when times got hard, and I remember him saying:

"Charles, if you go with me, I will show you ways to make money. You should walk down the alley with me and hunt for valuable things people throw away."

"I'll consider it," I said, "I do not think I would like to do it."

Taking no for an answer, Garry kept on asking me to go with him to get the exercise. I traveled down the alley singing and looking in trash dumps just to have fun with him. I looked for beer cans to cash them in for money and behind the Standard Service Station was located a dumpster, and I found a ten dollar bill, and I thanked Garry for letting me know people throw valuable house whole goods in dumpsters that can be sold or reused again.

Many of my articles and ideas for novels were written on the third floor, and I wrote into the early morning hours. While staying at the rooming house, I bought a black and white television in 1991 from the Good Will Store, which lasted for four years, and it showed good pictures. Even though living on the third floor was not what I was use to, it made me happy to be independent doing what I wanted to do. I did not like the idea of not being able to have an air conditioner and the only relief consisted of us using a fan which blew hot air.

When my stepfather moved into the house with us, he could not get alone with my mother, and I found myself getting to know him when he woke me up in the morning, and invited me to eat some of his cornbread, and black eye peas, and being a great fan of horse racing; he always betted on the horses. The major problem developed around his critical need for reliable transportation to get to the racetrack. He made deals with me to drive him and his friends to Fairmount Race Track located in Illinois.

On a typical night for horse racing, Willie said to me with a great smile, "Charles I want you to take me and a friend of mine to the race track and I will give you five dollars."

I said, "Willie that is not enough. Gas is costing too much money these days; I want at least $ 20 dollars."

This type of bargaining started a heated debate between me and him because he would bet $ 100 dollars on the horses to win and give me five dollars. When he saw I meant business, I got what I wanted to pay for gas expenses.

While staying at my address on Grand Avenue, I was a substitute teacher for the Normandy, Maplewood, Jennings, and Special School Districts, and I bought a 1977 Lincoln Town Car in order to get to work. When I went to the Normandy School District, I taught gym classes in the grade schools, and at Normandy High School. I performed the same duties for the Maplewood School District. At the Jennings School District, I taught social studies for a semester. I assisted another teacher and taught autistic children who worked hard to keep up with students who were not autistic at Washington Junior High. I taught social skills at Melville High School, and I remembered when a man came into the school auditorium, and spoke to the students about the dangers of cigarette smoking, he said doctors performed twenty operations on him to kill the cancer in his throat, and he pulled seven tubes out of his throat which he used to swallow his food with.

One of the fellows, who lived in the house, by the name of Slick, gave me a white trench coat which I still have. When my stepfather moved in to the house and rented a room; he cooked for me and the other fellows too, and I loved his corn bread. When I stayed on the third floor in my one room apartment, I wrote articles for newspapers and short stories and a novel which I will rewrite in the future. Joe, Joe the person who managed the apartment said using air conditioners was prohibited, but we could use fans. I remember many hot nights sleeping on the floor near the windows to keep cool, and I put towels in cold water and rubbed myself down with it. I met a fellow, who lived on the second floor, and he became a good friend of mine and we called him Sam because he looked like Sammy Davis Junior. At that time I competed in karate tournaments and twenty trophies I won in competition were displayed in my room.

Wanting larger space, I rented an apartment at 4037 Palm which was cross the street from my mother's apartment, and she lived at 4034 Palm. The desire to be free and independent kept pulling at me, and I wanted larger space with more rooms. My apartment consisted of a living room, kitchen, bedroom, and restroom. My neighbor Liz, lived in the apartment under me, and we became good friends. She wanted me to take her to the store to buy videos and even though she was big for her size, Liz showed a loving smile and we talked about feeding the birds.

"Charles I like feeding the birds and enjoy watching them eat and fight each other over food," She said. During the spring and summer months, Liz's family members and friends sat on the front steps and talked. One morning I came home and laid on the couch and when I opened my eyes after ten minutes of resting; I noticed a figure running across the living room floor. It appeared to be a rat and it scared me to death. In deciding what to do, I called a friend of mine by the name of Allen Berry and said to him:" Allen I need your help in getting this rat out of my house." I said, "Can I come over and pick you up? Maybe we both can kill him!"

"Ok man just come over and get me," Allen said.

When we got to my house, Allen looked into a cabinet and said," There he is. I'll try to make him run out of the cabinet." When all attempts to kill the rat failed, I bought a large rat trap to do the job. After putting peanut butter on it, I watched the rat trying to get the peanut butter and the steel device landed on him but he survived the blow and dragged the trap back into the cabinet.

"There he goes I shouted!" as the rat ran into the back of the stove, I said, "I'll light the oven and make him come out." Heat from the stove made him scramble out of it, and into the living room, with Allen and me in hot pursuit after him. I tried to hit him with mop stick, but I kept on missing as he ran back into the living room and under the couch.

"I'll move the couch!" I yelled.

The rat ran from under the couch and into the kitchen again with us trying to hit him. His feet made a heavy beat as he moved towards the kitchen. The apartment looked like a tornado demolished it. Table chairs and furniture were turned in different directions. Both of us tried to keep our breaths because chasing after the rat was exhausting, and when he left the room; I stopped for a rest in the kitchen. Allen jumped on a chair at times when we saw him. In the kitchen the rat came out and I took a deadly swing at his head and he fell dead.

"I got him!" I shouted to Allen.

The doorbell ringed and Liz thought we were fighting each other because of the noise made trying to kill the rat and finally I hit him over his head with a final blow. It was too dangerous for me to ignore this problem. Allen hit him again to make sure he was dead. Putting the rat on some cardboard, Allen threw him into the back yard and several of the neighbors came over to look at him.

Liz's daughter Stormy was nine years old and made the honor role at the grade school she attended. A contest was held at school and she competed in it, and won first place, and this involved students giving oral presentations. My mother lived across the street and I went over to see her when I was not busy. Willie Winfield was my mother's husband and we shared some good and bad times together in our relationship.

Kathy stayed in the apartment on the first floor and had three children and professed a love for Caribbean life styles. In any given day, Kathy wore braids and dreadlocks, and her major activities were taking care of her children. Her father worked and enjoyed running a lot. A fellow by the name of Joe and his wife lived in a house next to my mother's. When it was warm, family and friends sat on his porch and talked with each other. Most of the time I came over to

Joe's house, and we talked about my court cases as a prose attorney. An elderly lady in her nineties by the name of Lill stayed under my mother and was full of life. On Natural Bridge Avenue was located Fair Grounds Park which consisted of basketball and tennis courts utilized by many people who came over to use it. Included in the park was a pond for fishing activities, and enough land for baseball, and little league football. Many tall trees surrounded the park, and parents took their kids to the area where they played on the swings, and the park had a swimming pool. Many of the high school officials held tennis and baseball games in the park for their students. Knowing I was a diabetic, I walked around the park to reduce my blood pressure. Cory Sphinx who won three professional world titles in boxing was one of the fellows I met, when I did my running and I told him I practiced in the martial arts, and trained for tournaments in the park. When I walked in the park, I saw people in the community having affairs such as concerts, public speaking, and people from churches giving services, and social organizations giving seminars on different civic problems affecting their life styles. Sometimes I strolled through the park and looked at the geese eat grass, the squirrels running back and forth eating acorns, and playing with each other. Giving musical concerts was a major activity in the park, and on the corner of Natural Bridge and Grand the Aldi Store consisted of many customers coming in and out of it who participated in activities at the park. Since Aldi's prices were low a family with a low income could feed their families.

When stores like Aldi gave a cheaper price for food, it was a good thing for customers.

Many of my karate practices took place in the park which included Kelyan Bell, Raynard, Juan Davis, and me. One evening when it snowed heavily all three of us met at Fair Grounds Park and trained. Later Juan drove us to Lucus and Hunt Road and we ran through heavy snow for about six miles and came back and sparred with each other. At that time Kelyan was probably 21 years old, Raynard 26, and Juan about 24, I, 42, and I really enjoyed myself.

During that time leading to the late nineteen eighties, I spent three days at Ritenour High School and met a business teacher by the name of Terry Bunton and our relationship lasted for about eight years. I enjoyed her three children Lester, Lisa, and Lesley. To have fun, Terry and I discussed our teaching objectives because I was a licensed school teacher myself, and Terry gave me teaching suggestions many times during my teaching career. Working many years at the University of Missouri at St. Louis, as an administrator, Terry helped people get jobs at the university, and she cooked great meals for the family which I loved eating. With much interest in teaching, I saw her on a television program talking about education. Her daughter Lesley earned a Bachelor of Science degree in Journalism from the University of Missouri, Columbia. Basketball took Lisa's interest at Ritenour High School and she played on the team with other girl students. Lester's father spent time in the Navy, and Lester Jr did the same thing, and later he got married. When I substitute taught at the junior high, Lester was one of my students. One of Terry's relatives died in Milwaukee and Terry and I along with other members of her family drove up to Milwaukee for the funeral. All of us took turns driving. During the holidays, I enjoyed good times and memories with them. Terry was impressed with me trying to obtain a good education and encouraged me to always strive to be the best in whatever I attempted to do. The opportunity to meet her family made me very proud and they always treated me with love and respect. Some times for recreation, Terry and I went to the track field and walked around it trying to keep in shape. When my book got published," The Making of a Black Belt Karate Champion" my thoughts went back to the time some 10 years ago when her daughter Lisa said, "Just think what it would be like when Charles becomes a famous writer one day." That comment was brought to my memory, after I finished the book and saw it selling in many Asian and European countries all over the world. Most of the time, Lisa saw me reading books on writing or writing articles. I got a lucky break to write an article for the St. Louis Post-Dispatch and all of the family members left me alone in the dining room to write it and did not disturb me because this newspaper was the number one ranked paper in the city of St. Louis with millions of readers. Bad winters caused 68th Street much difficulty to drive through and I remember going to Terry's house helping the family to dig their cars out of the snow. Anything Terry could do to help her daughters and son advance their careers; she did it with counseling and financial support she gave with love and devotion. Her kids showed their love for her.

CHAPTER 10

TRAVELING AROUND THE VARIOUS UNITED STATES CITIES TO DO INVENTORIES IN THE EARLY NINETIES

In those early years in the nineties, I held a job as an inventory clerk, and I applied for it because they said I would travel to different states doing inventory work, and I got an opportunity to see some states in the western parts of our country. Being alone would not be a problem because I shared this experience with other people and got paid for it. We traveled to Kansas City, Missouri, Minnesota, Oklahoma, Wisconsin, and many other states. It snowed badly in Kansas City, Missouri, and the company paid for us to stay at a hotel and I bought a grey trench coat at a good will store to stay warm. It gets colder in the western states in September then it does in Missouri. For the first time in my life, I got a chance to see black squirrels, and it was a surprise to me because squirrels in St. Louis, Missouri are grey. While I stayed at the hotel in Kansas City, it gave me an opportunity to practice karate when the inventory was completed. When doing the inventory, groups of us were assigned sections of the store to use our machines to count the products. Keith was my roommate and he helped drive the van. Before leaving the company, we left our cars at the company site. Teamwork played an important role in doing our work successfully, because many of us looked up to the people in management, to help instruct us in the inventory work; we did not know anything about. While we drove to different cities, it was fun looking at places I had never seen before. The company gave us spending money to buy food when we did inventories in the cities we visited.

CHAPTER 11

MY YEARS AS A JOURNALIST 1984 TO 1995

When I was at Vashon High School teaching English, I attended Washington University located in St. Louis, Missouri and graduated with a Specialized Certificate on May 18,1984 in Journalism and a Bachelor of Science degree in that same area on May 17,1985. I interned at KMOX television under Julius Hunter and Bob Hamilton at KMOX radio, and wrote the evening news as it came off the teletype wires. When it came to professionalism, Mr. Hunter taught us gathering news for the broadcast aired on the evening news, and how they interviewed people to explain events taking place in their stories. To teach his class, Mr. Hunter used a book in which he was the author.

Taking his class to the news room was exciting and we watched him deliver news to the television audience. One important thing which Mr. Hunter stressed was for us to always be on time, when meeting people in the professional world of journalism, and he won many awards for his work, and contributed his time to many charitable causes helping the community in civic events, and gave royalty money to social organizations from his book called "Portland Place". I enjoyed his classes and will always remember him.

When I interned under Bob Hamilton at KMOX, I did not know about radio broadcasting, but when I left my internship under him;

I learned how to take news off the teletype wires which might be twenty inches in length and condense them into ten sentences so that Bob could broadcast the evening news live over the radio. It felt good hearing him tell your story as he explained the events which were taking place in the St. Louis community. When the news events came in, Bob showed me the techniques which were used to write the evening news. Writing the news to be broadcasted became exciting and I learned a lot. Sometimes I could thank Dr. Slattery for putting me in the writing lab for ten weeks because he hated my writing and said he would fail me if I did not go there and learn how to write better sentences. (Smile) News reporting became interesting when Roy Malone taught the class, and he cared a lot about his students, and met with them on days he did not have to work, to help with their writing projects. Our final research project was to get an article published, and I did an article for the Northside Journal on the car seat law for infants in the state of Missouri, and they published it. After that, I wrote several feature articles for the Northside Journal, and one of my biggest paying articles was when I did one for the Daily Record on a big building project in down town St. Louis. A faculty member by the name of Wendy Hearn taught classes at Washington University in the journalism department, and she did documentaries, and I enjoyed her classes; she was killed in an airplane crash, but I learned much knowledge from her teachings. Introduction to Journalism was taught by Jim Fox and he made us do articles on topics of interest such as sports, community news, or anything which was not being written about. For many years, Jim Fox wrote a column for the St. Louis Post-Dispatch.

My articles appeared in the St. Louis American, the Argus News Paper, the Sentinel, and the Beauty Time Magazine. I wrote feature articles for the Sentinel Newspaper on their "Yes I Can" award winners who contributed to the growth and development of the St. Louis community. The newspaper gave awards dinners to honor them. I gained experience working for the Sentinel Newspaper covering politics in the city, education topics, crime, and interviewed many civic leaders to write feature articles.

I did some freelance writing for the Beauty Times Magazine, and interviewed black customers, who shopped at their beauty supply stores.

One lady customer said," Charles they look at you as if you are going to steal something, and they do not take products back if they break up, and you cannot use them anymore. They do not have warranties on their products."

When writing for the Sentinel, I covered major events happening in St. Louis as a freelance writer. Sometimes I sold the same articles to more than one newspaper. Al Wallace, who they called Big City, wrote a column for the Sentinel News Paper on local politics in St. Louis, Missouri. Al was tall and slim and he smoked cigars. Instead of Al asking me for clips of my old articles before doing a writing assignment, he said," Pointer just go out and do the story."

This surprised me because most editors wanted to see clips of published work before they gave you an article to write for their paper. Mike Williams was in charge of running the newspaper, and Howard Woods founded it, and he passed before I got a chance to meet him. The Sentinel News Paper gave me one of my first brakes to get steady freelance writing assignments and I got paid for it.

Al said to me laughing, "Charles the politicians always called and asked me to save the newspapers for them so they could see what was being said about them."

Another person I would like to mention is Bob Williams and he took pictures of the people who were in my articles and a picture of me for the front cover of my book called "The Making of a Black Belt Karate Champion" which was published in March of 2012 by Xlibris Publishers. I tried sending articles to other magazines and received my share of rejections. Getting a good journalism education helped me to work on interesting topics which appealed to me and especially when I wrote my motions in court and did legal briefs as a prose attorney. My counselor Diane Willis will never be forgotten because she was there when I needed to speak with someone about my career objectives.

Some of the topics I wrote about were in the field of education for example, when the students in the Wellston School District did well on the BEST TEST for The North Side Journal and I did an article on The Meaning of Halloween for them also. Bob Williams took pictures of the Normandy School District band, and choir, and I wrote an article on them for the <u>North Side Journal</u>. In doing that article, I interviewed, the band and choir members, and people watching the concert under the direction of Mr. Bugs. When students said they were allowed to cheat on their assignments at the Wellston School District meeting I attended, I wrote an article on that too.

One evening I went for a job interview to apply for an English teaching position in a school district and the principal said as I showed him my articles, "Charles I've seen this article of your you are showing me."

CHAPTER 12

MY WONDERFUL FRIEND ETHEL

One evening I received a call from a dear friend of mine by the name of Ethel who I met in 1974 at the Sears building, and after shopping I rode on the bus and got off when she did. I later walked her home, and we went to the movies and saw John Wayne in a motion picture called "The Alamo." Fifteen years later in the early nineties, she called and left a message, and I called her back. We dated and visited each other's homes, and she counseled me on the problems I encountered, in my daily life. When we got together, we had fun and took trips to Marquette Park located in Grafton, Illinois. As you traveled down the highway to Grafton, the Mississippi River was to the left of you, and you could see people riding their boats on it. When people spent the night at the lodge, they stayed there as long as they wanted to and the food was tasty. Ethel was a nurse by trade; she graduated from O'Fallon Technical High School in the clerical department, and later went to nursing school for a year, and earned her LPN certificate. Her sister Gwen traveled a lot after she retired and Ethel sometimes went with her. When I litigated cases as a prose attorney, Ethel sometimes predicted what might happen in the decision making process, because she served on jury duty for many years. Encountering trouble trying to get admitted into law school, she always comforted me with words of encouragement, when I received rejection letters, after working two jobs to pay the application fees at the Special School District, and Office Max. To have fun sometimes, I went over to her house, and watched cable television, and played with her cat Mickey, who was spotted with black, orange and brown colors. For fun, I used my fabulous voice and singed songs showing her how much I appreciated our friendship, and left balloons on her door saying I love you. One evening Ethel came over to my apartment and on the couch was three African styled dresses I bought for her birthday. On all of the holidays she and I sat in the back yard listening to music and took turns watching the fire to make sure it would not burn up the food. Arguments took place at times but we always worked them out. Her son James came to visit and helped her with activities to repair things on her house. Being independent, Ethel handled her responsibilities regardless of how difficult it was to deal with them, and she and her mother Mrs. Rogers had a close relationship. When Mrs. Rogers got older and couldn't do for herself, Ethel went to her house and took care of the chores for her mother. Her relatives were close to her and Ethel enjoyed going to their family gatherings especially during the holidays. For pleasure, Ethel took trips with her friends. When I went to Columbia, Missouri Ethel went with me to watch me win a Gold Medal in the Missouri Show Me State Games in karate competition. She was also a constant companion when I attended the Concord online law school. I've known Ethel for at least twenty years and she will always be a great friend in my life. I developed a good relationship with Ethel's mother Mrs. Rogers who I spoke to many times when I called to see if Ethel was at her house.

CHAPTER 13

1990 TO 2000 YEARS OF CHALLENGE TO OVERCOME ADVERSITY

To still keep trying to get employment, I got a job at the St. Louis Job Corps Center located at 4300 Good fellow, in St. Louis, Missouri as a counselor which required a Master of Science degree in counseling education. After I earned my Bachelor of Science degree, I went an extra year and completed my graduate degree in June of 1975. The St. Louis Job Corps Center trained people in various trades so they could enter the employment world prepared and get skilled jobs to make a living for themselves. The group consisted of mostly high school drop outs and many of them graduated from high school, but wanted to learn a trade or get a paid two year education to earn their Associate of Arts degree in a field of their choice. Counselor's caseloads consisted of sixty or seventy students and the male counselors were in charge of the boys. The girl students looked for guidance from the women counselors, who always helped them with their social and personal needs, and inspired them to get their GEDS, and learn a trade, and possibly get into a two year community college program paid for by the Department of Labor.

With many students coming from different states, they sought opportunity to advance themselves. The students came from poor and middleclass families consisting of different ethnic groups. The students I counseled stayed in Dorm 53, and my employment at the center lasted from 1991 to 1993. My supervisor, Charles Fearn counseled me when I attended Forest Park Community College during my freshman and sophomore years from 1969 to 1971, before I graduated from that institution. Having a great personality, and pleasant smile, he appeared to have a height of 5'5". During the late hours when the students slept, night supervisors stayed up from 11.p.m. to 7a.m. watching them to make sure no unwanted strangers visited their sleeping quarters during that time period. Before getting trained in their trades, the students took a series of career orientation workshops in different career specialties to see which ones they wanted as a career objective that would give them much success.

Married with two kids, Daryl Todd enjoyed being a counselor, and he worked with me when counseling our students. When the counselors worked late into the evenings, Daryl cooked food on a small portable grill, and when he left the center, he lost a lot of weight. The counselors dressed in suits. At about 3: 00 p.m., the students assembled in a hallway where the RA, which meant residential advisors, did roll call. As a counselor, I sometimes came into the hallway and spoke to the boys to see if any of them needed help in any way.

A fellow by the name of Jumper became the RA on my floor. He tried to address the boy's needs, and he allowed them to talk with me if he could not help with their problems. To help the boys with their social problems, counselors performed one on one counseling sessions with each boy once a month. Group counseling sessions took place and we talked about the normal problems the boys faced as students adjusting to campus life. Many of the boys came from low income areas and some of them belonged in gangs before enrolling into the center. The fellows who wanted to be Bloods wore red clothing and the Cribs wore the color blue when dressing.

William Griffin, my residential adviser, organized the dormitory into a parliamentary system, and Kevin Warren who I constantly disciplined settled down and the students elected him president of the dorm. During the dorm meetings, the boys discussed many of their problems instead of not trying to communicate how they attempted to adjust to campus life. Anything positive the students wanted, I tried to get it for them. To be a counselor, a Master of Science degree was needed. To deal with the boys' drug habits, counselors and department heads met with Dr. Boyd, and we discussed information on students who needed help, and what would be done to resolve their habits with possible treatment. The center provided many activities for their students and one evening the music director gave a concert. The students provided singing; however, the concert was lengthy. As a way of keeping our boys on legal probation and not drift back into crime, Mr. Charles Fearn called me into his office and said, "Charles I have an assignment for you. I want you to take our boys up to the prison and let the prisoners talk with them. These talks may persuade our students to not violate their probation".

"Ok," I said, "I'll be back as soon as possible and tell you what it was like watching the prisoners talk with the students."

At about 12 p.m. five students came strolling towards the van, boarded it, and took a seat, and much joy came to them when we rode on the highway towards the prison. As we entered the room, five or six prisoners waited for them. At first they showed them a film of a man being electrocuted. The looks on everybody's face showed disbelief when they saw this taking place and the fear in their faces because this made many of them upset to see a man's eyes popping out of his face and his head being disfigured.

One of the prisoners said," The purpose of bringing you up here is to tell you if you do not obey your probation officer you may be placed in prison forever."

One of them said, "Prisoner life is not what you think it is because anything you want in the streets, you can get it in prison."

"Weapons are no problem to get in this place because we make our own without anyone knowing anything about it, and some prisoners are killed in here without a trace of who did it." One of the prisoners said.

One prisoner said, "The food in this place is awful because they put too much salt in it and if you get sick, it might take several days for you to see a doctor because he has over 600 patients to see."

With an ugly look in his face another prisoner said, "If you think your girlfriend will be waiting for you to get out of jail you are wasting your time, and you will be disappointed when you are released from prison."

The prisoners tried their best to put fear into the students' hearts to help them avoid the urge to restart a life of crime. I enjoyed telling Mr. Fearn about our experience going to the prison, and I think this discussion influenced many of the boys not to violate their probation while at the St. Louis Job Corps Center. On the ride home the boys stayed quiet, and talked very little about what they saw in the discussion about living a life of crime.

While I was at the St. Louis Job Corps Center, I trained with the students at the age of 41 in karate to get to know them better. The students were 20 years younger than me, and our sensei Terrill Williams taught the martial arts to them. After many years of training, Sensei received his black belt from Ernest Hart four time world champion. Sensei Williams' rank in karate is seventh degree Black Belt. In his classes, Sensei Williams taught all of his students to be humble, and we said a pledge after each class session which was: In the art of open style karate I will always display a humble attitude in my never ending search for perfection. I will always give one hundred percent of myself and I will do nothing to disrespect my class, my family, my sensei or myself. Many of the students I counseled participated in the karate classes, and they treated their counselor just like anyone else, with love, and respect for each other. A handful of the students came from broken homes, and Sensei Williams and I taught them against joining gangs, doing drugs, and living a life of crime. Winning a trophy in karate competition meant much to them, and it showed with hard work they could be productive, and complete their trades, and earn their GEDS. I never assumed the responsibilities of representing the karate students at a discipline committee meeting for violating campus rules, because they did not want to get into trouble, and tried to make their counselor and Sensei Williams proud of them.

After training for six months, I took part in a karate tournament with my students, and won the first place trophy, and at a dorm meeting my residential advisor presented me with the trophy in front of the boys I counseled in Dorm 53, and they gave me a standing ovation. While I worked at the center, I competed in the karate tournaments for two years, and after I left in 1993, I won over 60 trophies, six Missouri Show Me State medals, a Budweiser National Championship trophy, a finalist medal in the US Open World Karate Championship held in Orlando, Florida in Disney World, and I placed in the Blue Grass Nationals held in the state of Tennessee at the Gualt Hotel. Recently I just won a third place trophy at the 35th Southern Illinois Karate Championships on March 20, 2012 given by Mark Varner, and the second place trophy at the St. Louis Silver Sundown Karate Tournament on May 19, 2012 hosted by Sensei Terry Creamer at the age of 62.

The Karate Championships I Participated In

1992—Sig Gees 12th St. Louis Open Kumite Men's White Belt Heavy Weight Division—First Place Trophy,

1992—Jefferson Davis Presents the 12th Annual St. Louis Budweiser Karate Classic—Kumite, White Belt Men's Division—Second Place Trophy

1993—16th Southern Illinois Championship October 2, 1993—Third Place Trophy, Kata, Fighting—First Place Trophy

1993—St. Louis Karate Spectacular, October 1993, Directed By Karen Ensor, Julia Pusateri, Fighting—Second Place Trophy—Second Place Trophy in Kata Competition

1993—Jefferson Davis Presents St. Louis Budweiser, the 13th Annual Karate Classic 1993—Third Place Trophy in Kumite

1994—17th Southern Illinois Karate Championships 1994, First Place Trophy in Fighting

1994—Haussner Presents 8th St. Louis Karate Championships, First Place Trophy in Fighting First Place Trophy in Kata

1994—Terry Creamer Presents St. Louis Silver Sun Down, Saturday, May 1 4,1994,Second Place Trophy in Fighting

1994—American Karate Co CA Cola Classic, Third Place Trophy in Kata, Senior Advanced, Second Place Trophy in Kumite, and Second Place Trophy in Weapons.

1994—To 1997—Missouri Show Me State Games, Won Two Bronze, Two Silver and Two Gold Medals

1995—Jefferson Davis Presents St. Louis Bush Beer Summer Karate Classic, Second Place Trophy in Fighting, Second Place Trophy in kata

1995—November 15th Annual Budweiser Karate Championship Directed by Sensei Davis, Third Place Trophy in Kata and Second Place Trophy in Fighting

1995—Hauser Presents 9th St. Louis Karate Championship, Second Place Trophy in Fighting

1995—American Karate Coca Cola Classic, April 22th, Third Place Trophy in Fighting

1996—Lou Millers 7th Shorin Ryu Pro AM Karate Tournament, October 12,Third Place Trophy in Fighting Black Belt Seniors 35 to 42 Years

1996—19th Southern Illinois Karate Championship, March Third Place in Fighting

1996—Jefferson Davis Presents 16th Annual St. Louis Budweiser 1996 Karate Classic September, National Black League Outlaw Conference SKIAAA Rated, Second Place Trophy in Fighting

1996—Blue Grass National Finalist Karate Championship, Medals in Fighting and Karate

1996—Midwest Regional Karate Championship, First Place Trophy in Fighting

1997—Kellie Hausner Presents St. Louis Super Star Open, Second Place Trophy in Black Belt Kumite Senior Division

September 1997—Rick Norton Battle of St. Louis Karate Championships First Place in Fighting

1997—7th Shorin Ryu Lou Miller Pro AM First Place Trophy in Kata

1997—March 23 The Central Missouri Martial Arts Association And USA-KIA United States All Style Karate Championships, Third Place Trophy in Fighting

1998—the Midwest Regional Karate Championship, Second Place Trophy in Kata, Second Place Trophy in Fighting

1998—Sensei Davis Presents The 18th Annual St. Louis Budweiser 1998 Karate Nationals Classic, September 26th 1998,National Black Belt League Outlaw Conference SKI Sanctioned AAA Rated Second Place Trophy in Fighting, Third Place Trophy in Kata

1999—US Open Finalist World Championship Medal, Orlando, Florida, Disney World, Point Fighting

1999—Blue Grass Nationals, Finalist Karate Championships Medals in Fighting and Kata

1999—American Karate Classic Championship April 17, 1999, Second Place Trophy in Fighting

1999—22th Southern Illinois Karate Championships, March, Second Place Trophy in Fighting, Third Place Trophy in Kata

2000—23th Southern Illinois Karate Championship, March, 16th, 2000, Third Place Trophy in Fighting, Fourth Place Trophy in Kata and Weapons

2000—20th September 22-23 Shihan Jefferson Davis Presents 20th Annual St. Louis Budweiser National Karate Classic National Black Belt League Great Plains Conference Sponsored By Grey Eagle Distributors, Third Place Trophy in Kata, Creative Forms,

Third Place Trophy in Traditional Kata, First Place Trophy in Fighting Winning The National Championship

2001—11th Annual Shorin Ryu-Pro AM Second Place Trophy in Kumite Division, Black Belt Seniors, Light Weight June 2, 2001

2001—Shihan Jefferson Davis Presents 21th Annual St. Louis Budweiser National Karate Classic, Second Place Trophy in Fighting

2001—Terry Creamer All Star Karate Academy Presents. St. Louis Silver Sundown Karate Tournament, May 5th 2001, Second Place Trophy in Fighting

Another counselor I would like talk about is David Swingler, who we called Swingman, he inspired many of his students to achieve higher heights in whatever they tried to do that was positive and me, David and Greg Anderson another counselor, all grew up in the hood, and the students could identify with us because they saw we came from the same low income environment, and did not let that defeat our desires to go on to college and achieve success after we earned our degrees. One evening Greg and David watched me run around the track field at Beaumont High School, when I prepared for a karate tournament. Both of them possessed unique personalities.

As a result of that experience with the students, I wrote a book called "The Making of a Black Belt Karate Champion," published by Xlibris, March 2012.

CHAPTER 14

EARNED A BACHELOR OF SCIENCE DEGREE IN CRIMINAL JUSTICE 1997 TO 2001 FROM THE UNIVERSITY OF MISSOURI, ST. LOUIS

When I worked two jobs to pay application fees for law school, I did not get accepted by any of them, and it cost over $1000 dollars, but I took a look at the situation, and decided to go on to the University of Missouri, St. Louis, and take criminal justice courses to see what aptitude I possessed in law. When applying for admission to the law school, they never told me why I could not be admitted, but I did not let that discourage me. The program in criminal justice ranked number one in the nation, and I found that challenging, and decided to get a foundation in law first. Writing played a major role in many of the courses I took under Dr. Scott, who taught the administrative law courses, Victims Of Crime, and Communities and Crimes, and during these classes, he wanted you to take part in discussions which the students did in open class. There were a variety of subject matters, and sometimes we talked about crimes which were committed in the community, such as the case of the criminal who the police placed in the back of their police car and he dislocated his shoulder, and managed to get his hand cups off, and grabbed a gun, and shot a policeman. The policemen who captured the criminal, and placed him in handcuffs felt he was not a threat to them, and they failed to check the suspect to see if he had a weapon he killed the policeman with. I wrote papers on Girl Gangs in St. Louis, Security in the School System, and a paper on the success of the Dare Program, sponsored by policemen.

Learning about the juvenile justice system presented interesting topics in this area of study especially when we discussed when juveniles could be certified to stand trial, and what happened when they became older, and if the crimes they committed were dropped after they reached adult age. Under another professor who taught criminal law, I learned about the different types of crimes like burglary, rape, arson, murder, assault, and battery, the death penalty, parole, freedom of speech, and many aspects of crimes. This professor became a judge in the city courts in St. Louis, MO. One lesson he wanted us to learn was to be able to discuss the law in any conversation when meeting people in an intelligent fashion. I enrolled in a class called Seminar 390, and I chose my topic to be DNA and The Death Penalty and I interviewed people to get their opinion on if they thought DNA should be used to test people accused of serious crimes before giving them the death sentence. After collecting the data from the interviews, I performed, I put the data in a formula to get results, I enjoyed this project very much. I ran into some problems doing the project because I could not meet with Dr. Carsgrove to get the final ok on my paper. His son was constantly in and out of the hospital because of his diabetic condition. I went to the computer lab, and they helped me finish the project and I earned a B on my paper. My good friend Reggie and I took some classes together, and we enjoyed associating with each other. Sometimes I called him while I took my law courses from Concord Law School on line over the internet. I had a good time in my criminal justice classes and I was excited about graduating from the program. When I took Introduction to Criminal Justice, I taped the lectures because the instructor gave many pages of notes. I always referred back to the taped lectures which helped me get a good grade. Taking Theories of Crime showed me how law enforcement people solved crimes, and the difficulty in doing it. After three years, I graduated on May 19, 2001 with a Bachelor of Science degree in Criminal Justice, and I made the Dean's List with seven A's, three B's, and one Ct in all of my courses. By going to the University of Missouri at St. Louis and earning my degree in a law related field; it showed I was smart enough to enter a law program, because I ranked high in criminal justice from a number one ranked university in the United States in that subject area.

CHAPTER 15

MY TRAINING AS A PARALEGAL AT FLORISSANT VALLEY COMMUNITY COLLEGE

Trying to gain more knowledge about law, I went to paralegal school, and studied for four years to earn 64 credit hours. The courses I took were taught by attorneys. My earlier courses; ethics, real estate law, introduction to paralegal studies, and legal writing were taken at Webster University where I received a grade of D but enrolled in it under a judge, at Florissant Valley Community College and received an A. At Florissant Valley Community College, I took courses like evidence, employment law, administrative law, and business law, law dealing with goods and services, and mediation, and arbitration. The thought of going into their paralegal program presented problems because my employment during that time was not steady, and I worked at any job I could find to take care of myself, and dropped out of school several semesters because of the lack of money, and made arrangements to put half of the tuition money down, and finished paying the rest of it before the semester ended. One of the last courses I took was called Computers, and the Law, and I did not have a computer to work with. To complete my courses, I did my lessons in the computer lab, and I felt with hard work, and determination I could take this course and graduate. Before going to Florissant Valley Community College, I went to Meramec Community College and took the course Computers and the Law, and hated it because the white students did not speak to me, and two white instructors taught the class. The younger instructor did not want to explain things to me, but the older lady instructor embraced me with open arms. When problems developed, she met with me during her spare time and gave me much advice to improve in the class. Walking into the class, we were told to form groups, and all the white students got in groups, and I was left standing in the middle of the floor trying to figure which one to get into, and the older instructor said, "Charles you are in this group."

One black female in the group acted as if she could not speak to me. I think much fear developed with the white students because a Kirkwood police officer became the victim of a black man who shot him. Years later a black man came into Kirkwood City Hall and the news casters said he killed about eight or more members of the city hall council members. I remember doing a class project for our group, and went to the various department stores, and did an inventory on different computer parts, and turned it in to our group so we could all get credit for the project, and when they saw how professional it was typed, each of them came to the back of the computer lab, and thanked me personally. At first, they did not reach out to me to join their group. Being much older, working, and studying with different racial groups never became a problem. To graduate with 6 degrees and a specialized certificate, I sought the help of all races of people who could help me reach my goals. I judged people by the content of their character instead of what race they were. To achieve success in life, people of many races will be there to help you, and I experienced this first hand, and professor Chiles who was Caucasian, paid for the figure drawing course I took when I first enrolled for college. His wife later told me he came from a poor family, and understood what it was like to have nothing trying to get a good education, and when he saw I grew up in the low economic areas of the black community; he wanted to see me get a good education, and he and Mr. Jones felt proud of me when I graduated from college with my Bachelor of Science degree in Secondary Education with a major in Social Studies and minor in English, and my Master of Science degree from Southern Illinois University at Edwardsville in Counseling Education.

CHAPTER 16

WHAT IT WAS LIKE BEING A PRO-SE ATTORNEY

What led me to representing myself in court came by accident, because I did not know anything about law, when I felt something should be done to get relief from the court when my rights were violated. Taking on the big lawyers without any legal training became exciting, and sometimes a nightmare, and a learning experience I'll never forget.

Making mistakes became a way of life. The Constitution said I could represent myself, but it did not say how much hell I would have to go through in the process. Sherry, another Pro-Se said, "The only thing judges hate is Pro-Se litigants do not follow civil procedure which irritates them."

Most of my research was done at St. Louis University and Washington University Law Schools, and the exciting thing I liked about that law library was reading case law, and seeing how judges used the law to make decisions. Most of the comfortable moments of my life took place when I studied in the law library. I drifted into a discipline; I knew little about. This situation placed me not in a law school, but the real thing of litigation because not knowing what strategies to use to defeat the other attorneys made me lose the case.

When I took my first course in criminal law under attorney Mullens, I enjoyed his class, because he introduced us to many aspects of criminal law. Clerks in the law library helped me when searching for information for my cases. At first, I made mistakes in writing petitions, and barely survived getting dismissed, but I studied the opinions of the judges closely. What prompted me to litigate my own cases was I could not afford an attorney, and I got tired of being abused, and not being able to stand up against injustice.

Many judges and attorneys showed prejudice and bias against the Pro-Se's representing themselves. One individual by the name of Judge Seltzer did not want me to talk when presenting my case to the court. After going over my motions and looking at the manner I presented my pleadings he said, "Mr. Pointer you know how to represent your case in this court." The clerks told me representing yourself was a fatal mistake. I earned six degrees, and a specialized certificate, and school officials at Washington University Law School did not tell me why I could not attend their law school, but the United States Constitution said I could practice law, and represent myself in court. This section of my book brought out the best in me, and having faith in God to challenge and face lawyers who attended law school in St. Louis, MO and I was not given this opportunity when I applied to several law schools.

In Pointer v Home Depot No.4; 04-CV-103-1031 CAS, one of the lawyers by the name of O 'Harris wrote Judge Shaw a letter and said I gained much experience by me doing litigation in many discrimination cases, and he wanted me to have the same legal expections as he and his lawyer associates when I used a legal term called Construct Validity to attack one of his motions to get my case dismissed. By attending paralegal school, doing my cases became much easier, because lawyers taught me valuable lessons in the classes, which I used arguing against opposing lawyers.

I'll try to summarize some of the cases I litigated as a prose attorney, such as the case Pointer v. En banc Order NOS: 09-1564/1620, issued by nine justices of the Eight Circuit Federal Court, stating I filed meritless and frivolous petitions, and I appealed to the Eighth Circuit Appellate Court, saying I did not get notice the en banc order would be issued to me, so I could object and give reasons for opposition, and nine judges said I abused the legal system, but they did not say specifically where in my petitions I wrote frivolous information in them.

Sherry, another Pro-Se, advised me on those points I raised in my appeal. The appellate court judges said the nine federal court judges tried to stop me from using the courts to file my petitions, and felt they violated my civil rights. Doing the appellate brief posed difficult problems for me, because the judges in the appellate court wanted me to consolidate two cases into one, and write one showing where my rights were violated. Now, I can file my petitions in court without having to do these eight unconstitutional measures first when the appellate court ruled in my favor. Federal judges are appointed by the president of the United States. I fought for what I believed in, even though I was not allowed to attend law school in St. Louis, MO, which has two of them.

Another case called Pointer v. Ida Early etal (4:2009 cv 014370) found itself on the United States Supreme Court Docket NO; 10-8446, March 21, 2011, when Ida Early secretary to the Washington University Board of Trustees opened my mail when I wanted the board members to check into why I could not get admitted into the law school, when law school officials never told me why, which I felt was an inference of discrimination. I felt the lower courts made many mistakes because it is illegal to open people's mail without a search warrant and not forward them to the people it was intended to go to. Five or more United States Supreme Court judges voted for me to have my case placed on the docket in January of 2011, and they denied it cert in March of 2011. My friends told me I should be proud of myself, because it was an honor to be placed on the docket to be reviewed, because my case was given a second chance to be finally examined, and especially with me not being a licensed attorney. Many lawyers send briefs to the United States Supreme Court and are defeated in their attempts to get their cases placed on the docket. Writing that brief became a problem because the clerks at the court made me rewrite the brief several times before it went before the justices to get permission to place it on the docket, because the rules are strict, and I did not have anyone helping me write the brief, and some lawyers get companies who specialize in writing briefs for the United States Supreme Court to write it for them.

In <u>Pointer v. Dart NO-04-2425</u> I defeated a well-known attorney when he filed a motion for summary judgment and Judge Hamilton granted me some attorneys after I defeated his motion for summary judgment. I spent three weeks in the law library getting case law to use, and cited the Rules of Evidence to oppose his determination to defeat my case where it would not go to court. At first, when I called this lawyer he would say, "Why are you calling me? Go get yourself a lawyer." and laughed at me. His paralegal never gave me any respect when I called and treated me the way he did. This lawyer defeated me in a motion to compel, and I wanted him to give me information for my case, and when we were in court he said," Your honor it's the manner in which he wrote his questions is what I do not agree with."

Judge Hamilton explained how she wanted me to write my questions in my motion to compel. After that experience, I said to myself," I'll be ready the next time when he tries to get my case stopped before it gets to trial and if they could have given me an opportunity to attend law school, to learn how to write motions to compel, getting my petition written would not have been a problem." Attending paralegal school was not thought of at that time. To prepare myself, I studied tons of law books in the law library, and prepared my opposition brief, and turned it into the court on time. In about two weeks, I received a call from Judge Hamilton, and the other attorney was on the phone, and she said, "Charles, how are you today?"

I said, "Ok Judge Hamilton."

She said, "The other attorney is on the phone, and have you received my decision on your opposition to summary judgment?"

I said, "No, Judge Hamilton."

"Mr. Pointer I've read your opposition paper; you have survived summary judgment, and I will assign you some lawyers to take this case to trial. Your new lawyers will get in touch with you in a few weeks because you will need them."

I said, "Thanks your honor."

After the conversation with Judge Hamilton, I jumped into the air and shouted. Trying to write in a cold house posed difficult problems for me but all the hard work paid off, and with the help of God, I wrote in my little room with a heater, but the rest of the house was cold. In a meeting with my new lawyers, the lawyer I defeated in summary judgment said, "It was in my wildest dreams a non-lawyer would defeat me in summary judgment." The next time when I called the opposition lawyer, his paralegal spoke to me with so much respect when I telephoned their office for information. We probably would have won the case, but Judge Hamilton did not let our witnesses testify to say they did not influence my supervisor to fire me, keeping me from getting my promotion. I spoke to the probation officers, and they told me they did not have anything to do with telling my supervisor to fire me, but he said they did. My attorneys took the case to the 8th Circuit Appellate Court, and the judges ruled I was discriminated against, but they could not rule against the findings of trial court. The girl who got the promotion did not have a Master of Science degree like I did in counseling education, and all of those classes I took required the instructor to have a PHD. The case was denied cert in the United States Supreme Court, but I gave it my best, and I was proud of that, and I learned many valuable things about litigation and the law.

One of the other cases I litigated started when I sent my money order through the mail to pay my gas bill, and someone intercepted it, and cashed it at the Naval Federal Credit Union in Fairfax, Virginia. I filed the petition in the small claims court, and in Fairfax, Virginia, and the defendant refused to appear in court, and I won on a default judgment, and received a little over three hundred dollars for damages. I lived in a cold house as a result of my money order being stolen, and cashed at the Naval Federal Credit Union.

In the case <u>Pointer v. Architecture Metals</u>, a supervisor kept harassing me but he did not bother the two white fellows who worked with me, and they had less days on the job then I did, and we later settled for a nice amount of money to keep from going into a lot of litigation for the two days I was harassed. The fellow doing the harassment was African American. "Because he did not discriminate against the other black employees does not mean he cannot discriminate against Pointer," Judge Perry said. Opposing counsel disrespected me and said he did not have to shake my hand when I greeted him with courtesy. I later wrote a letter to the firm's partners about this prejudice treatment. I had no dealings with him after that.

In <u>Pointer v Clean Serve No: 4 CV-981 SNL</u>, I filed suit in court because the company did not give me a raise and review according to their employee hand book, and when I asked them about it, they said it would be on next week's paycheck, and I never saw any raises on my paycheck, and when they fired me, I went to court, and we eventually settled for a cash settlement. It was a breach in contract because their employee handbook said I was supposed to get a raise and review every six months, but they did not honor the contract so I took the issue to court.

In Pointer v. The Missouri Division of Corrections, No. 0-023047, I passed the state written test for corrections officer, and the job required a high school diploma, and I possessed a Master of Science degree in Counseling Education, and did not get hired, and I took the case to the 8th Circuit Federal Court who remanded it back to Judge Limbaugh saying I was discriminated against. After viewing the case in the lower federal court, he dismissed the case and said I marked the EEOC box saying age discrimination instead of race discrimination as the reason the Department of Corrections did not hire me. I did say in the petition it was an inference of discrimination; I did not get hired when no non-discriminatory reason was given for not hiring me. I could have appealed his decision a second time after I studied for a year at Concord Law School which was on line. I did not have the legal training to know what to do at that time I litigated the case.

I took the state test, and passed it, but they refused to hire me saying I had felony and misdemeanors charges against me, but I was able to prove lies were said about these charges, but they kept my name off the list of eligible candidates.

I did oral argument in <u>Pointer v. The Department of Social Services,N0 ED 90301</u> when the official did not give a justified reason for denying me energy assistance in the 22 Missouri Appellate Court, and I lost because I did not appeal the decision of the administrative agency before trial court made its decision. When I was a student paralegal, my lawyer professors always told me to appeal the lower court decision when sending a brief to the appellate court, and this is what I did in this case. In class, they never told us about appealing administrative agency decisions, and I learned a valuable lesson from this experience because I will remember this if I finish law school, and become a practicing attorney in the future.

I did oral argument in the 22th Missouri Appellate Court in <u>Pointer v Venita Washington, ED86169</u> because of child support issues when she took my kids to another state, and did not tell me anything about it, and I asked for a temporary injunction to keep the state from getting my income tax money because she did not let me see my children, and the 22th Missouri Appellate Court said I should have asked for a permanent injunction instead. Much emotion was shown because I paid the child support, but I could not see my kids, and today they are grown, and I have not seen them since they were 21 or 22 and that was eight years ago. Some relief came from the court in their decision when they said a law indicated that child support stops when the non-custodial parent is kept from seeing their children. I took family law, and that bill was never discussed, and I told my attorney about it. Doing oral argument taught me much about discussing legal issues before the appellate court, because you have to explain your points to the court and write a brief which requires much research, and use good clarity in your writing, so the judges will know what is important in your appeal, you are trying to get justice from.

Other cases, I litigated were <u>Pointer v. Parent For Fair Share NO-02-1335, Pointer v. Special School District No: 00CV 1874 ERW, Pointer v Building Stars, NO 04-2146, Pointer v Building Butlers, 04-3518, IN RE Charles Pointer NO-08-1387, IN RE Charles Pointer 4:2005MC00658, Pointer v Home Depot No: 4:04 CV1031 CAS</u>

I filled out a computer application at Home Depot and was not hired by Ernie, who made the decision to employ other people. I hurried to the back of the store, and spoke to Ernie, and he said he would check on the status of my application in a few days. Trying to find out what he said about my application, Ernie said, "I cannot tell you."

Being upset, I chose to file a complaint with the Missouri Commission on Human Rights. The the main problem with this case was Ernie did not give me a non-discriminatory reason for not hiring me. By studying case law, I used a precedent case called <u>McDonnell Douglas v Green 411 U.S. at 802-04,</u> which set the standard law for hiring and firing and that case took place in St. Louis, Missouri, and the ruling came from a United States Supreme Court case. I felt Ernie owed me a non-discriminatory reason for not employing me, and an explanation as to what is was I did not answer correctly on the application. With my experience employed as a former sales associate, getting hired by Ernie seemed to pose no problem, and he would give me gainful employment, because I waited on customers, and assisted them when selecting their products at Office Max. Not only did I have experience in sales, my academic background indicated I took courses in business management, accounting, introduction to business, and business law. The upsetting thing Ernie did was hire people after I did not get considered. Having perspective applicants take exams, and employers do not give notice they will not be considered for employment if they marked answers they did not like violates the Fourteenth Amendment of the United States Constitution. Notice must be given to the applicants filling out the application to answer the questions properly so it would not hurt them when seeking to get hired. I did not find out the reason defendant did not hire me until opposing counsel sent me some discovery materials. Interpretation of the scores posed questions for me, to understand what they stood for, with proper meanings, so an applicant could see where they made their mistakes, which kept them from getting the job, he or she applied for. The court and defendant said I did not qualify for any of the jobs which were available, but no qualifications were listed to measure my abilities, to work at Home Depot. Critical circumstances resulted while this dilemma with Home Depot took place, because my gas was turned off which caused me mental anguish. Difficult times set in, which made it hard to write in cold weather with a small heater to keep me warm. To get relief from the court, I wrote the 8th Circuit Appellate Court, and requested an extension to turn in my brief, because of the cold living conditions in my house, and that I could not complete it on time. My gas utilities were off. I sent correspondence to counsel requesting we set up a date to discuss discovery questions, which I wanted him to consider, dated July 29, 2005. In an effort to stop me from winning my case, counsel did not turn in my entire discovery requests for admissions, interrogatories, and production of documents. All of the new people Home Depot hired were not trained in the various trades, and many of their new hired employees were not trained in those various trades where materials were sold, and they received orientation training before going on the sales floor to sell hardware supplies.

Key questions were asked in discovery which showed defendant was hiding valuable information when I sent them my discovery questions such as the following taken from DEFENDANT HOME DEPOT U.S.A.;INC'S ANSWERS TO PLAINTIFF'S FIRST SET OF INTERROGATORIES

Question 8 Was applicant told what type of qualifications Ernie agent for Home Depot looked for when hiring new people?

Response: Home Depot objects to this request on the grounds that it unduly vague and ambiguous, overly broad, unduly burdensome, and seeks information that is neither relevant to claims raised nor likely to lead to the discovery of admissible evidence.

I was not hired but I never saw any qualifications for jobs which the company said they had.

Question 9 Are people trained for positions when they get hired?

Home Depot objects to this requests on the grounds that it is unduly vague and ambiguous, overly broad, unduly burdensome, and seeks information that is either relevant to claims raised nor likely to lead to the discovery of admissible evidence. Subject to and without waiving this objection, Home Depot responds as follows: yes.

To respond to this question, I would say there were people hired who got training to perform the job, and I should have been given the same opportunity.

Part of the case McDonnell Douglas v. Green 411 U.S. at 802-04 was that a non-discriminatory reason must be given for not hiring a new applicant and defendant kept hiring people after he did not hire me.

In HR Guide to the Internet EEOC Disparate Treatment, I used the following to oppose counsel saying in McDonnell Douglas v. Green 411 U.S.at 802-04 a non-discriminatory reason have to be given as to why a perspective employee was not hired which said Direct Method—Burden shifting

1 These cases McDonnell Douglas v. Green U.S.792 (1973) later refined in Texas Department of Community Affairs. Burdine 450 U.S.248 (1981) and St. Mary's Honor Center v. Hicks 509 U.S. 502 (1993) the analysis is as follows: This is a direct method:

1 Plaintiff must establish a prima facie case of discrimination(2) the employer must then articulate through admissible evidence a legitimate non-discriminatory reason for its actions (3) in order to prevail the plaintiff must prove that the employer's stated reason is a pretext to hide discrimination McDonnell Douglas.411 U.S. at 802-04

When I did not get justice in the federal court, I appealed to the Eighth Circuit Appellate Court. I attacked opposing counsel's efforts to use an en banc order to make me file leave of court every time I sent a law suit to their court. To confuse the issues, opposing counsel tried to influence the panel of judges to rule in his favor.

I sent in an interrogatory question asking what the requirements were for taking in shopping carts and counsel did not answer the question, because I saw a person whose only job was to take in shopping carts. With no requirements for the job, I could have been hired to do that.

I filed in forma pauperis when filing motions in court. To let both parties know what their obligations to this case were, Judge Shaw wrote out a case management order. Opposing counsel wrote a letter to Judge Shaw stating I had much experience in handling these cases, and wanted me to live up to the same standards as them, and to litigate all of this case in a legal manner according to the Rules Of Federal Civil Procedures. The court ruled against me, but did not rule on the fact notice was not given on if you did not answer a question to Home Depot's liking you could not be considered for the job. I was not told by defendant why I did not get the job. I was not given an interview to see if I was qualified for jobs which were open. I saw African American bringing carts off the parking lot and I felt you did not have to have experience to do that. I did not have a copy of my answers to see if they changed them on the computer. No evaluation was given to say what was wrong with my application, and placed in writing for documentation purposes.

To summarize, I felt Home Depot did not treat me fairly because I should have been interviewed, and hired just like the other applicants, to find out about conflicting issues which might affect my chances of getting hired. The responses I made could be changed on the computer when I filed a suit against them, to reflect I did not care about the needs of the customers, who asked for help, when trying to shop at their store.

Pointer v. Special School District No: 4 00CV1874 ERW

One year was spent working at the Special School District as a teacher assistant, and they sent me to Westchester Elementary Grade School. Before being sent to Westchester, I worked at Newowner, Melville High School, Lewis and Clark Elementary, and Washington Junior High. One evening while I graded papers in another part of the room; Miss. Blosser and an 11 year old student were having a physical confrontation with each other, and she asked me to help her escort Willis out of the classroom, which I did. Actually, I was not part of the incident, just a teacher responding to Mrs. Blosser asking me to help with a troubled student. Mrs. Blosser and I both escorted the kicking and screaming student out of the room, and down the hallway to another room, where he calmed down. While Willis waited in the room, he attacked me and finally he settled down. I did not touch the student. While Mrs. Blosser and the principal of Westchester were in their room a meeting was arranged to meet with Willis's parents to get to the bottom of everything to see what took place in the confrontation between Willis and his teacher Mrs. Blosser. The area coordinator called and told me not to come to the meeting which I explained in my petition. I felt this was disparate treatment against me because I did not have a chance to explain my side of what took place when Mrs. Blosser and Willis were having their problems with each other, and was not invited to the meeting. In my petition to the court, I explained how the school officials had meetings with each other, and I was not invited to any of them, before I was dismissed. School officials placed discipline reports in my folder; I knew nothing about, and my signature was not on any of the papers to say I received them. The documentation they placed in my file was defamation of character, and misrepresentation, because they made carbon copies going to Dottie instead of me. This form of litigation is concealment by defendant. While working at those four schools, I never received any negative evaluations whatsoever. Before going to court, I thought I was paying a person who was a lawyer, and I found out she did not appear in court, and she was not a lawyer, and I lost money as a result. The appointed mediator said I was being used as a skate goat because I did not do anything wrong to lose my job. School officials placed the blame on me to keep Willis's parents from suing the school district, because the teacher was an adult, and Willis was a minor. All of this was in the petition and opposing counsel did not produce any evidence I did anything wrong. They did not follow the guidelines of their employee handbooks which is a breach. The person according to their employee handbook must be a given chance to improve before being fired, but I did not get that opportunity. Fraud correspondence was placed into my folder attempting to show there was a continuous flow of communication between me, and school officials with me doing wrong all the time. I never had seen the documents before. If this was true, why did they keep sending me to different schools after I completed my assignments? The case was taken to the 8th Circuit Federal Appellate Court, and I lost and was denied cert in the United States Supreme Court. It would be cheaper on the school officials to get rid of me and place the blame on me. I did not do anything wrong to lose my job. If I was not allowed to work during the investigation, Mrs. Blossor should have been done the same way. They violated Rule 56 where documents were not certified by the court. The biggest problem I've seen is that Missouri employers rely on the at will doctrine to win employment discrimination cases.

Pointer v. The St. Louis Board of Education 400cvo 187 ITIA

I taught at Vashon High School from 1981 to 1984. The school was located on Grand and Bell. The housing projects were located in the back of it. Being built in a low income area, large amounts of traffic traveled on Grand Avenue on the side of the high school. To the south of Vashon, the Fox Theater hosted many top broadcasting shows, and visitors ate at the Steak House, and in attendance were many out of town people, and college students, and citizens living in the area. After two years of getting bad evaluations, and complaining I did not get enough training, I was suspended pending a hearing which was not given to me. The teacher's union representative did not advise me of my rights and the importance of going to a hearing. Since I stayed with Venita and we had a newborn child on the way; I resigned from the St. Louis Public School System, and got my pension money, which I felt was a great mistake. I kept asking for a hearing date and I resigned instead of getting fired. This event had a great impact on me and my family which made it difficult for me, and obtaining a job became a big problem, because of bad references from the school district, and at that time Venita became pregnant. I took immediate action, and filed an EEOC complaint in 1984, feeling I was discriminated against, but nothing happened. In my petition, I said the personnel department did not hire me because I filed an EEOC complaint against them, after I resigned in 1984 without being given a hearing. Disparate treatment, I felt took place when they attempted to recruit people from South Africa, when it was difficult for them to teach with their accents.

My application was rejected when they said they would get back in touch with me. Missouri law indicated a hearing before the school board must be given before terminating a teacher. Many teachers were resigning from the field of education in St. Louis, and in addition to that, I explained they advertised there was a shortage of teachers in their school system, and felt I should have been hired.

A large amount of people going to college at that time stopped seeking a career in teaching, and sought other occupational fields to go into, which paid more money, with less headaches dealing with teaching students. When they kept teachers who were charged with possession of drugs, I felt they could have hired me back because I did not have drug charges pending against me. Two teachers in the system had drug related problems but were hired back to their teaching positions. In 1981, the school board laid off people who they felt was not certified in their teaching fields, and I was one of them. Before this took place, I went to the University of Missouri, St. Louis and completed my certification in English grades 7-12, and felt I should not have been laid off. For two months, I sat at home, and the other English teachers received training in a new English curriculum called Essential Skills of English. This unlawful action I felt was discrimination or disparate treatment against me. The certification division for the state of Missouri sent me my certification after they received my transcript. Certification officials forwarded my teacher's license back to me and I took this information to school officials after two months of complaining. They school officials called me back, and told me to report to Vashon High School in October of 1981. After two years of bad evaluations, I requested a transfer because the same people who evaluated me unfairly in the first year did it the second year too. When I kept getting bad evaluations, I requested to receive training but was ignored by the school officials at Vashon High School. Later I was suspended pending a hearing. To get legal representation, Judge Alderman appointed attorney George Washington Graham to do some prose work. James C. Hytlage represented the St. Louis Board of

Education and their firm was called Lashly and Buer, P.C. 7114 Locust Street, St. Louis, MO 63101. The joint proposal scheduling plan was submitted on March 28, 2001 and signed by attorney Hetlage and me. Discovery was completed and the school board won the case.

Pleadings Filed In This Case:

1   Defendant's First Set of Interrogatives Directed to Plaintiff.

2   Defendant's Answers and Objectives to Plaintiff's Second Set of Interrogatories

When I went to the Eighth Circuit Court of Appeals, I did not know anything about writing appellate briefs when appealing the lower court's decision. I did not have money to pay an attorney to write one but I felt I could present something to the court representing myself. Each time I wrote a brief, I got better at it. When writing this brief, I was ignorant of the legal process and did not have experience in this area of law. My cover page was not written the way the Eighth Circuit Court required it to be, which is more detailed then the Missouri State Court of Appeals for the 22nd district.

Included in this brief were the following: Table Of Contents, Jurisdictional Statement, Statement of The Facts, Points To Be Relied On, Cases Used, Argument And Conclusion, and included in this section is a copy of my response to their brief.

My critique Of Judge Adelman's Memorandum and Order section,

When looking at the discussion, I felt I was qualified when Judge Alderman listed three examples to prove a prima facie case of discrimination:

I filed a charge of discrimination against the school board in 1984. In Exhibit B the computer printout said no probable cause was issued. A charge was filed. The judge said I did not file an EEOC complaint, but according to the computer printout I did. There was an adverse action taken against me. They did not give non-discriminatory reasons for not hiring me which falls under <u>McDonnell Douglas v.</u> <u>Green.411 U.S.at-802-04</u>. There was a causal connection between the discrimination charge and adverse employment action. At first they prepared me to start teaching and later they stopped without a non-discriminatory given reason for it. Miss. Stewart gave the first go ahead, but later Miss. Johnson sent me a letter saying they would contact me, but hired other people afterwards because of the job fairs. The only problem is they hired other people with fewer qualifications than me. It was brought to their attention a copy of the computer printout of the1984 decision was printed and sent to me but was ignored when it was presented in my appellate brief dated August 20, 2002 page 65. To summarize this case, I am saying the court failed to see I filed a claim of discrimination in 1984 which the agency said they were burned. The first court did not question the issue of defendant not giving a non-discriminatory reason for not hiring me which is a violation under Title 7 of the 1964 Civil Rights Bill. The issues to the litigation were printed on the computer printout stating an inference of discrimination took place because Mrs. Stewart was going to hire me, and Miss. Johnson intervened, and sent me a letter saying they would contact me, if they were interested in employing me as a teacher.

In Pointer's brief, he said disparate treatment took place when the school board trained other teachers in Essential Skills of English, and not Pointer, who was kept from working for two months without being paid and up to this day, I haven't received my back pay. They violated statute 168.124 which said Board may place on leave provisions governing the board of education of a school district may place on leave of absence as many teachers as may be necessary because of the decrease in pupil enrollment, school district reorganization, or financial condition of the school district. I kept calling school board officials for a hearing date and none were given and I resigned. The committee of people who evaluated me consisted of the same members the second year. I requested a transfer, and the personnel office would not give me one, but I knew of another teacher who requested one, and got it when he knew he would be evaluated unfairly.

Missouri Statute 168.011 said teachers must be certified but many of their teachers were not fully certified in their teaching fields, but allowed to teach the students and two of them were in classes I took, when I attended the University of Missouri, St. Louis. This was one of the reasons the school board lost its accreditation.

Pointer v Riverview Gardens NO-05-1567

From December 2001 to January 2002, I substitute taught for the Riverview Gardens School District as an English teacher. Seeing the students used black dialect and slang in their written and oral communication, I wanted to teach the importance of using standard English in the business world. I looked for books at the Julia Davis Library on that topic and found an album called "Dialect of the Black American" designed to encourage people in the business work world to use standard English when dealing with professional business matters. The students identified with the contents of the album because they listened to black slang in their rap music. One part of the album showed an appellant did not get the job because he used black dialect in his interview. When I played the album, a white female teacher came into the classroom and asked me to turn the volume down which I did. When she asked for me to do this, an ugly frown appeared on her face, and she did not look too happy when she said it. Later Miss. Montgomery came into the classroom and sat down, and the students were quiet, and listened to two minutes of the album. A student brought a note to me from Miss. Montgomery and I went to see her. She said I was no longer going to teach the English classes. School officials told me I could teach the English classes until the end of the school year. Miss. Montgomery told me she received some complaints from students, but failed to identify the students, or what the complaints were about. Miss. Montgomery said my students came up to the door before the bell ringed but other teachers allowed their students to do this. Many teachers did not permit it. I was told by Miss. Montgomery the students were given planners saying students could not stand at the door before the bell rung. When I started teaching, I was not given a planner to know about any rules telling me what I could do or not do. In a court of law, I could raise the issue that notice was not given to me about the rule in the planning books the students were given. I did not have as much knowledge about the law at that time to argue this issue.

The students enjoyed listening to the album. The word Ebonics was not written on the album and Miss. Montgomery said I did not explain what the album was about before it was played. How could she make a statement like that when she only came into the class when it was about to end? No one in the school administration listened to the album to know what it was talking about before saying I was teaching Ebonics. The speakers who produced the album were not teaching any foreign language. No one gave me an evaluation on my teaching methods so how cold they say I was not meeting school expectations? The lessons I taught came out of the books they gave me and later they changed some of the books, I used to teach my classes. School officials did not care if a change of books affected the guidelines of the curriculum guide or not. They were only concerned about getting books to the kids. It was not my goal to teach from books outside the curriculum. The dismissal came when I played an album which talked about the differences in standard English, and how black dialect related to it, and standard English should be used in the business world. Even Miss. Rosen fell said I was teaching Ebonics, and she never heard the album. I feel I was discriminated against and not given proper training like Mr. Stewart was when being introduced to a new reading program, and he was a white person. At least three people who were white sat down and trained him on teaching the new reading program. I being African American was not oriented or briefed about the curriculum guide or how to use it, plus they changed my literature books. I feel sex discrimination played a role in their attitude because there were no black male English teachers in the English Department. To summarize, Missouri is an Employment at Will state and if you do not sign a contract of employment they can fire you for any reason so long as its non-discriminatory. There were some non-Title V11 claims in this case but at the time I did not know anything about the law like I do now after taking my paralegal courses, which were taught by lawyers and completing torts, criminal law, and contracts at Concord Law School, an online law school.

I was later terminated from the job. At the same time before I substitute taught as an English teacher, I applied for a teaching position as a regular English teacher and I did not get hired. Another male English teacher who was white got the position and he had a provisional certificate in English. The newly hired English teacher told Mr. Stewart this when all three of us were in the classroom. I was certified in grades 7-12 in English for life.

I helped Mr. Stewart grade his finals. I was not briefed on the use of a big 300 page curriculum guide. The English department head said if I needed any help just ask her. Mr. Stewart or Miss. Montgomery never told me how to use the binder and Mr. Stewart was too busy preparing his students for their final exams and I assisted him in this effort. He was helped by four people who were white to organize and teach the new reading materials. There were computers in the room and he was trained in using different programing materials to teach the kids reading. I was not briefed on what to teach in the curriculum book. Mr. Stewart gave me my books to teach the composition and literature classes.

A case management order was issued by the judge after I filed a complaint under Title V11 and discovery took place. I did defendant's request for documents, interrogative questions, and admissions, but they failed to answer my interrogatives which were sent to Mr. Stewart, Mrs. Montgomery, and Miss. Rosenfeld. The termination letter said I was not a fit, which I felt meant because I was black, and male, I got terminated from my job. No non-discriminatory reasons were placed in a letter stating why I was fired. This case was tried by Judge Perry who ruled in favor of defendant. The court upheld fraudulent practices by letting defendant submit a list of students who were not in the classroom when Miss. Montgomery listened to an album called "Dialect of the Black American" who could say he was not teaching Ebonics. I was defeated in summary judgment motion and filed an appeal. A brief was written by both sides and they ruled in favor of appellee. I did survive judicial review when the judge told me to separate my non-Title claims from Title V11 claims. I felt bias was shown when she said I could get another judge to try the case. The appellate court only affirmed the lower court but did not address anything about the case. Attorney Lawrence tried to influence the other judges because she sent them the en banc order saying I had to sign leave of court every time I filed my petitions in court. I wrote that the prejudice effects of the case outweighed its probative value. The attorney and I fought this case for several years. At the deposition, charges were brought against me after I filed my petition not while I taught at the high school. The album was designed to encourage students to use standard English in the business world. The goal of every English department is to make sure its students are prepared to write in English because it is the accepted standard form of communication. No evaluation of my teaching abilities was ever done on me so how could they say I was a bad teacher. Other teachers used supplements to teach their classes like I did. Miss. Montgomery did not read the album cover before accusing me of teaching Ebonics. I did not have any certification in teaching Ebonics. The appellate court dismissed the case but refused to let attorney Lawrence used the en banc order against me which showed prejudice against me to make me do eight unconstitutional measures before filing my cases in court. My First Amendments rights were violated but after taking courses in the paralegal classes on employment law, I realized they felt I was an employee at will and could do anything they wanted to do to violate my rights, but they did not think I would take them to court for it. Being a substitute teacher, you have no protection to keep from being discriminated against.

CHAPTER 17

MY JOURNAL COVERING LITIGATING CASES AS PRO-SE ATTORNEY

<u>June 6, 2000</u> My kids are trying to communicate with each other now that they are grown adults. Kalah my youngest daughter is attending Joplin Christian College. I wrote and told her how proud I was to see she's trying to get a Christian education and I hope she can be happy with her choice. I told her she could be a journalist in her chosen field by writing books, doing screen plays, or articles on Christian life, or she could work for a Christian organization. I told Benica she is making me happy on her decision to follow in her father's footsteps, and be a writer, and taking correspondence courses from a school. My kids sent me a picture album of themselves, and I enjoyed looking at them, because I have not seen my daughters in six years and their mother concealed them from me most of their childhood lives. With them being much older, they tried to call me when time presented itself. Because of financial problems my marriage was broken up, but my children were not told the truth as to why it ended, but when they grew into adulthood; I explained the reasons why a divorce took place which made them very angry about it.

August 23.2000 Litigation under Judge Frawley

I went to a hearing to have child support terminated because Venita took my kids to Colorado. I arrived at 8:30 a.m. but Venita had not appeared yet. Judge Frawley did not let me speak about the laws I used to defend my position.

He said, "I know the law," when I attempted to speak. He denied my request without writing an explanation why and said I did not write out the memorandum correctly citing a Missouri statute. I requested a final order and judgment but Judge Frawley refused to give me one with no explanation. After that, I went to the cashier's office and requested documents for a Notice of Appeal because I needed a final order and judgment to appeal his decision. The deputy sheriffs told Judge Frawley what I wanted. I went back upstairs after I spoke to a court clerk in Division 1 which was Judge Grady's court, and she told me to go up there to see if anything had taken place. After Venita came thirty minutes late, Judge Frawley made his decision without hearing both sides of the issues from the parties in the case. The deputy sheriff said Venita came thirty minutes late after I left. In a court, I must be able to confront my accusers. I learned this much later when I took my law courses.

I was employed by a company called Clean Serve and helped clean a warehouse and office rooms at a dye company. I got to know a security officer by the name of Pitman who recently got out of the service, and he told me the company he worked for treated their officers very good as employees. I called Ed, the manager of security at Wackenhut, and asked if they could beat the salary I made at the other security company and he said yes and I traveled out to Clayton, MO, to the St. Louis County Police Department and got my license. I interviewed with Tom the manager for security hired by Wackenhut at the building I would later work at. At 4444, I met many people like Amy, part Indian married to a Chinese person. The unique thing about Amy was her ability to debate with me. Her long hair came down to her back and what made me speak to her was when she greeted me with that beautiful smile. When Amy walked by the officer's post I said, "I would like to say thank you for always giving me such a beautiful smile every time you pass by here in the morning."

Every time after meeting her we debated on many topics. When we talked about science, Amy knew much about that subject matter and she possessed a Bachelor of Science degree in Science and worked in the Genome Sequencing Department. We both agreed on doctors using stem cell research but she did not like lawyers and I credit her with getting me prepared to argue my cases before the 22nd Missouri Appellate Court. Conservatism from Amy always disagreed with my liberal viewpoints and she felt I wasted my time using the taxpayer's money by going into court representing myself. I'll never forget the good times we shared when debating with each other. The two of us started talking as she strolled by my post and before we reached the elevators she or I challenged each other in heated debate but it was mostly done in fun and I enjoyed discussing many things with other people too. Many times the different departments left food for security officers when they gave seminars at 4444.

CHAPTER 18

2000 TO 2007 CHARLES GETS A HOUSE AT 4774 MAFFIT

After graduating from the University of Missouri in 2001, I found myself having to leave the four family flat on Palm, and I learned the landlord sold it to another company located in Kansas. The new company said they would give each of us $ 500 dollars to move out. It was an exciting time of the year and my buddy Kelyan came home from the service on leave and helped me move. Getting a U-Haul truck, we stayed up most of the night moving my things. Using funds from my income tax money and teaching at Thurgood Marshall Charter School, I paid $ 2000 dollars down on the house when they required $ 1000 dollars. Ethel said this was a great achievement because I lost everything I owned in two divorces including my home on Count Drive. It was a blessing Kelyan came home to help me move my things and did not charge me anything. I enjoyed the fact that this house was in my name and no woman could put me out of it if things in our relationship made us break apart. On my old house which I lost, I planted pine trees which grew very large, and I did the same thing when I moved to 4771 Maffit. I threw out some grass seeds to grow a lawn, and painted the steps a dark purple color, and the attic was the length of the house. The living room consisted of three walls painted white with dark brown paneling. The sofa and love seat had matching dark blue pillows. After weeks of saving some money, I paid for a dining room set with a long table, and cabinet and I filled it with white china. To make the house look classier, I bought mahogany curtains to match the carpet, and designs ran through the curtains. Getting money from several law suits I litigated; I bought a new living room suit, a bedroom suite, stove, refrigerator, lawn more, and water heater. The bedroom set was black with gold trimming, and I placed new gold curtains in it and I put a leopard colored spread on the bed with orange and black spots. My study room consisted of white painted walls with new green curtains with beautiful designs, and I placed my lab top in that room. I painted the outside porch a white color and the basement walls white. I painted the side of the house with a light green color, and the front trimming, became a white color for the windows and doors. To complete the kitchen, I put a table with chairs in it, and years later I placed new tiles on the kitchen floor. The porch was painted white and my next door neighbor Lieutenant taught me a lot about cutting grass, and planting trees, and he insisted that I water the plants, and I remember him saying to me, "You are always making it look pretty around here."

Lieutenant owned a two family flat, and a one hundred year old two story house with many rooms in it. To the west of my house lived Miss. Purdue and her two daughters Van and Tina. Big Mike owned a two story house and he sold food from a truck going to different streets in the neighborhoods in St. Louis. Having no problem with transportation, Mike owned several trucks and cars and in many cases he repaired them himself. When I moved into my house a good friend of mine by the name of Robert, who did about twenty years in the armed forces, helped me and Kelyan move heavy furniture into my house. Being a small person, Robert weighed about 140 pounds and when my gas was turned on, Robert brought me some beans and skins to eat, and he loved to drink beer. Ken lived down the street and he brought the mail to us each morning. This set of people became very special to me because I communicated with them most of the time and Charley 82 years old and still living, who lived next door to Robert, told us about his years serving in Japan and World War II, and all three of us shared many good times talking about our life experiences. Robert told us about his experiences as gunner in a helicopter during the Vietnam War. My daughter got a chance to see my house and felt very proud of what I accomplished, when everything was taken from me in those divorces, but my pride and courage to never give up overcame the hurt I suffered from it. My daughter saw I defined what I wanted to do with my life, and not let the loses in my two marriages get me down, and not let it keep me from achieving success in whatever I wanted to do. Another friend of mine by the name of Tommy became a good friend while I cleaned floors at the dye company, and he told me about his experiences in Vietnam, and after work, I took him to the store and later home.

One evening Charlie, Robert, and I went to get some food from the pantry, and a car speeded towards us, and Charlie stopped his car just in time to avoid an accident. Much of my time was spent talking with Robert and Charlie, and we shoveled the snow off of each other's sidewalks in front our houses, and helped each other fix our lawn mowers when they broke down. To make money, Robert and I passed out leaflets informing people we would cut their grass for a reasonable amount of money. At that time a driver hit my car, and I contacted a lawyer, who later got me some money for my injury, and his name was Melvin Smith, and he helped me in another accident when a driver hit my car.

CHAPTER 19

2004 TO 2012 WORKING IN SECURITY AT WASHINGTON UNIVERSITY'S SCHOOL OF PHYSICAL THERAPY AND OCCUPATIONAL THERAPY

After working at Century Security, I got employment at Wackenhut Security and it took two summers and two years to get my Bachelor of Science degree in criminal justice, and I desperately wanted to get a job in my field. On the day of my graduation, my car needed repairs badly; I could not make the graduation, and I didn't have the money to buy the cap and gown. Still trying to in get a job in security, I managed to obtain a job with Century Security. The requirements to take a test and study in one day did not seem to bother me that much and I passed the test and got my license. All security officers sat for eight hours and people were taught various requirements to do the job of security officer. In my first assignment, they sent me to a trucking company, the YMCA, and a facility for senior citizens. At the trucking company, I stayed in the parking lot and got bitten by insects.

All kinds of people came to the YMCA and the people used devices to let guest in and sometimes rough looking characters showed up to visit residents living in the building.

The residents at the James House consisted of senior citizens, and many of the older ones shared with me what it was like to live in the 1920s up to the 2004. I worked there for three months and lost my job because someone lied and said I was sleeping at my post.

At 4444, I greeted guest who needed to find people who worked in the building, or opened doors for the cleaning crew, or construction people, needing to get into offices. The building housed the occupational therapy and physical therapy departments. Our supervisor Tom worked in journalism, and I told him about the articles I wrote for the newspapers, and he said he studied this subject matter in college. Jason, Vicky, Manuel, Johnny, Sandra, Eddie, Steve, and I were African Americans who worked at the Washington University campus, and each of them had unique personalities. To advance his literary skills, Eddie wrote poetry and entered contests. Johnny taught wrestling at Eastside High School. Vicky kept food at our desk so we could snack on it. Sports became a passion for Steve, and he always looked at the college football games, which he enjoyed a lot. Being a loving mother, Sandra was a wonderful person to work with and her father Lee passed away several months ago, and he and I enjoyed some good times talking about sports, and we debated on different topics, and I attended his funeral when he died.

Not only did I work with some incredible fellow officers, I met some students who I conversed with such as an African American named Keith, who was completing his last year of graduate school, in the doctoral program in the physical therapy program. After earning his Master's degree in Mechanical Engineering, he decided to earn a doctoral degree in physical therapy. Keith and I talked about the martial arts a lot and he said he practiced karate and indicated he would practice physical therapy in his home town of Memphis, Tennessee. To use his mechanical engineering degree, I encouraged him to try to make various designs of helping devices for physical therapy patients.

I met a student from Norway by the name of Magnus, and at that time he was completing his doctoral degree. I mostly saw him coming from the lab after gathering the results of many of his experiments.

The winter of 2005

During the winter of 2005 my gas was turned off because of over charges of child support coming out of my check. The gas bill was $1700 dollars and this situation became a large problem. Attempts at getting energy assistance were difficult because the officials said I made too much money, even after the child support was taken out. To prepare to keep warm, I bought a small heater, and my mother lent me some money to get another one. Most of the time, I brought the two heaters into my bedroom when the temperature went down. Even in the bedroom with the doors closed, it took two hours to get it warm, and to complicate matters, I wrote my briefs in coldness of the house, and used cold water to bath with. I managed to keep the electric on by going to Father Bobs and paying twenty five dollars, and they added fifty five dollars to it.

Before getting money for the light bill, Father Bob gave service and went over the scriptures. If there was a need for food, people received food from their pantry. During the month, I went to get food. My lady friend let me stay at her house. Several attempts were made to get Venita into court to have the support modified, but it became impossible. The last court order did not lower the $250 dollars child support in the last decision of 2005. When your body is cold, you cannot function too quickly, when you have to move about in the house. My toes ached a lot especially when cold weather touched them. Living in the cold affected my belief in God to bring me out of this dilemma which caused me to pray.

Ethel came down and assisted me in putting some plastic on the windows in my bedroom and spreads on the windows. Regardless of the circumstances, I paid the mortgages on my house, and I did not miss a payment. What little money I obtained, I used it on important things. Sometimes I used a grill to cook my food on and my mother bought me a blanket to keep myself warm. I hated these living conditions but I got use to it. My kitchen drain clogged up making it difficult for me to use it but I heated water to wash myself before going to work, and took showers at Ethel's house, and spent many nights sleeping there. When warmer weather set in the drain unclogged itself. The people at the energy assistance department did not do a good job in determining if I could get service when I took them to court. Many years later that agency was closed for not using the money to properly help the people with their needs.

On June 11, 2006, the child support organization sent me a letter stating $250 dollars was being reduced from my back child support. This was a great day in my life because they realized they overcharge me and it took three court visits to get some type of reduction of what they took from me, The organization decided to investigate my daughter's late start into college, and she did not go right after graduation, and I never saw any transcripts of her college work which was against the law to conceal this information from the paying non-custodial parent.

June 19, 2006 Jury Duty

I received a letter telling me to report to jury duty which became my first time doing it. Up into now, I never served in that capacity in the legal system. I got up early in the morning and the scheduled time of 8:00 a.m. presented no problem for me. Getting involved in jury duty offered a chance for me to see what lawyers went through when selecting everyday citizens to judge the rights and wrongs in a law suit with plaintiff trying to show defendant did him wrongs and he sought justice from the courts in return. It was important to be able to select the right kind of people for jury duty. All the people entering the court passed through the front entrance and were screened for guns, knives or anything which could be used as weapons. Next, the deputies told you where to report to once clearing the check point and sit to hear your assigned juror number called, and later a group of them are walked over to the court across the street by a sheriff. The lawyers representing their client asked the jurors questions and listened to their responses to see if they would be a danger to their client getting a fair trial. I answered some questions and asked one of the lawyers if photographs would be black, white, or colored. When taking evidence, my law professors said colored photographs could cause prejudice because it gives a more realistic affect. The lawyer asked if any of us were involved in accidents and I said yes I was and if any of us were trained in legal work and I responded, and told them about my criminal justice degree, my prose work, and taking five years to get my degree in paralegal studies. They did not select me as a juror, and I did not ask why but the jury consisted of mixed races of people.

August 1, 2006 Hearing for Work Mans Compensation

Today I got dressed and went to a hearing for a Workmen's Compensation claim. Mr. Klug greeted me in the lobby of the Workmen's Compensation Court.

"Mr. Pointer I cannot give you legal advice." Mr. Klug said.

"There was a breach of contract, "I said, "They promised me a contract if I stayed with the kids, teach them, and promote them to the sixth grade."

I showed Mr. Klug the prescription I paid for after I taught at their school. We were summoned into Judge Ottenad's chambers, and he and I spoke about the case. On May 12, 2002, I went to the clinic, and they took my blood pressure after I left Thurgood Marshall, and it increased to a high level. To settle the case, Mr. Clug said his client offered $ 200 dollars, and at first I thought about it, and accepted with $ 100 dollars going to child support. The money I got from the litigation helped me pay for a course called Dispute Resolution. In litigation I knew in many court cases, I could lose and not get any reward money. I went away feeling good I would be able to pay for the course. I passed of all my students and even the ones who gave me bad discipline problems. I spent a lot of time with my students and never gave up on them, when they ran away all their teachers except me.

August 2, 2007 Writing a United States Supreme Court Brief

Writing the United States Supreme Court brief presented many problems to me because of the great detail involved in completing it. I found myself constantly looking for papers and titles of cases to use in the brief. The brief showed how Office Depot employment personnel denied me the right to be employed, and I felt it was wrong, because I did not see any job postings or their qualifications, to see if I qualified for the job. In the process of writing the brief, I lost the papers which said August 24, 2007, giving me 90 days from that date to mail it. Last year when the Eighth Circuit Appellate Court made their decision, they took longer than ninety days to send it to me; I gathered all the information, and sent correspondence back to them saying I needed a date to use, so I could send the petition back to them in ninety days. I searched the folders for that document with no luck. Looking at all the work which was done, I felt unhappy. Finally, I looked at a book on writing resumes, and when I turned the page, it was located in the book on the night I was supposed to have it post-dated, and one of our employees did not come in on time, and got there at 11:45 P.M. instead of 11:00 pm. When she arrived, I left and drove to the post office, and the clerks helped me post marked it for the 18th of November.

January 17, 2007

After working Wednesday from 11.p.m. to 7a.m. in the morning, I decided to go to McDonalds and get me a cup of coffee, and an Egg McMuffin. As usual Mohammad, a light complexed tall African American spoke with me. Other fellows were up there too, especially when coffee was given out free on Monday's. After finishing my coffee, I went home and got to work organizing documents showing where energy assistance officials denied me service. My hearing took place in July of 2006 at the state building. For two winters without any heat I decided to do something about it, after being denied energy assistance. I wrote a letter and requested a hearing, which I attempted to explain to a hearing officer, why I should have been given energy assistance in the first place. When I came to the meeting, I thought it was on child support, and prepared a document to address the issue, but to my surprise, the hearing was on energy assistance. On the paper indicating where the meeting was to take place, the letters ER were at the top of the paper. I did not know what they meant. I asked the hearing officer to set a new date but he refused. I said most of Miss. Green's papers were inadmissible because she did not send me copies of the documents; she brought to the hearing, so that I could contest them. Missouri law indicated documents from the agency should have been sent to the other party which was me. The hearing officer who was a lawyer kept denying my pleas for inadmissible evidence. Many misrepresentations littered the documents Miss. Green used to deny me energy assistance. The law governing what Miss. Green did showed nothing in her tabulations. Instead of telling me I could appeal the hearing officer's decision to the board of commissioners, to give an advisory answer to the agency denying me assistance, I could later take the agency to court after this. I filed papers in the circuit court, but a clerk said the state agency did not send them any correspondence concerning the transcripts of the hearing and what was said, and after studying my law books; it said I could appeal the hearing officer's decisions, and on January 17, 2007, I sent the documents to Jefferson City for that purpose. On January the 18, 2007, I went to the public library and discussed strategy with Bob Williams. One of the biggest bills was the gas utility. It was difficult trying to live in a cold house because you developed into either a bitter person or one who is determined to succeed against all odds. The agency said I made too much money, which was presented by Miss. Green's tabulations of my income. During the winter of 06, I did not have any heat but the electric was on. To keep warm I bought an electric heater and placed it in my room and closed the doors. I placed plastic across the windows and put blankets on my bed. My mother was very helpful in that she always found encouraging things to say, and helped me buy a heater for my room. Her support will be remembered, and I was grateful she helped me. Everything I did in my house took place in my small bedroom which contained many of my cases. I represented myself in court as a prose litigant. Being a diabetic, I found it difficult to eat the right kinds of foods, because I was use to baking my meals. At first, I bought a grill and cooked my food, but I got tire of frying it in a cold house. To better things, I bought a portable hot plate, and cooked my food. At first I kept going to fast food places and grew very tire of it. When your house is cold, you do not think in terms of keeping the house tidy, because you are busy trying to survive, and keep warm. Many of my briefs were written for my court cases when I had little or no heat in the room. I dressed in warm clothes and studied at the same time. When you are faced with that type of adversity it makes you look at life differently. I did not wish this ordeal on anyone, and I felt people should be treated fairly in any situation, regardless of how it affected their livelihood, or standard of living. I dealt with the elements, and tried to keep from losing my mind, at the same time. The pipes froze keeping running water from coming out of the faucets. With it being cold in the house, I did not invite people to come to my house and who would come to a person's house, and it is cold inside of it. Nevertheless, mother, Kelyan, Carla, and Ethel came to the house.

One evening I went to the library and Bob Williams was speaking to a group of people.

"Charles I and these groups of people meet up here to see if we can help each other out." Bob called this group The Coalition for Justice. When I wrote for the North side Journal as a freelance writer, Bob took pictures of the Normandy High School Choir, and I wrote an article on the successes of the group, and the awards they won doing concerts

I told Bob about the problems I was having trying to get energy assistance and I wrote a petition to sue the energy assistance officials, because Miss. Green, who worked at the Human Development Corporation misrepresented my income, making it appear I brought more money home then I made. Miss. Green did not take into consideration that huge amounts of over charges of child support was taken from my check keeping me from paying a $ 1700 dollar gas bill and medical bills. Two months ago after the meeting with Bob and the coalition in January of 07; we wrote correspondence to the Board of Governors to appeal the hearing officer, and the Director of Family Services Janet Luck's decision. The attorney who works with the Board of Governors said, they do not cover those types of issues dealing with energy assistance.

Bob said," Charles we'll have to write him and find out who do we write."

I later received a letter showing agencies I could get help from and I called HDC and told some higher officials about the misrepresentation made by Miss, Green. I received phone call from Miss. Staling, and I explained the situation to her. Later Miss. Williams called me and I said, "Could you please look at the file to see how she wrote I made $ 1260 dollars on both checks. Later Miss. Williams checked the records and saw that I was correct and they gave me energy assistance, and later my gas was turned on.

Ethel helped me out because I stayed at her house when it was too cold in mine. Dirty a little kitten, which was born last year and left in my backyard, became a constant companion, after her mother left her and went away. Dirty sported a white and brown coat, and could stay outside for hours but sometimes I brought her into my room so she could stay warm. She came from a cold outside to a cold inside of my house. With the heaters blowing, Dirty always got in front of them and went to sleep. One evening I fed Dirty and went to sleep. I thought everything was ok, and I heard some noise in the corner of my small room, and there she was stealing some cat food chow out of the bag, and I threw a pillow at her, and she ran under the bed. By her eating too much food would make her sick. I told Robert, Mike, and Sherry about my success of getting the gas turned back on. Later I received papers of an entry of appearance from an attorney but I'd responded to a motion, and asked for a continuance, and no response came from the court, but I decided to attend the hearing any way on March 23, 2007. Judge Wilson said a clerk made the mistake of indicating the trial court date was May 23, 2000. I later found out it was on November 26, 2007. I spoke to Cherry and she said I must file a first amendment petition.

June 9, 2007

Kelyan called and said he was quitting his job because they wanted him to keep pushing the freight, and he felt he was not getting his required rest. I encouraged him to call the owner and get his job back. I told him he could not get his unemployment checks, if he walked off the job. Kelyan called the owner of the trucking firm, and said he was upset, and did not really mean to turn in his resignation and he wanted them to reconsider hiring him again. The owner told Kelyan to speak with the safety manager to see if they would rehire him.

September 26, 2007 Writing a United States Supreme Court Case and Preparing to do Oral Argument in the 22th Missouri Appellate Court

I've begun working on the United States Supreme Court brief on Pointer v. Home Depot. No 4:04-CV1031 CAS As I can see it, I tried to work on certain parts of the brief first. I worked on the statement of the case and why the writ should be granted. I am trying to see how the three judge panel of the Eighth Circuit Appellate Court conflicted with the United States Supreme Court cases and the 7th Circuit Appellate Court, to see if they would grant me cert in the case. I wrote the statement of the case, and reasons for granting the petition, and the constitutional statutes which should be used. I am using the Fourteenth Amendment, USCA 1981, and the1964 Civil Rights Bill. It's a difficult process because they denied me cert so many times. I guess I liked the challenge of seeing if I could get cert. I enjoy law so much because of the goal of trying to influence the judges to rule in my favor.

Tomorrow I embark on a journey to get a legal file done so I can make oral argument in the 22th Missouri Appellate Court of Missouri on energy assistance. Judge Wilson did not hear all of my issues on his motion to set aside the judgment.

In court I kept telling him, "Your honor I am being denied my 14th Amendments rights of equal protection of the laws."

November 11, 2007 Looking up a legal file problems developed for me attempting to retrieve it for an appeal against the state of Missouri Energy Assistance Department. On November 1, I went to the Julia Davis Library looking for Bob Williams, and his friend Rodney, but they were not in the library, when I went to see them. On November7, 2007, I called to see if the file was ready, and they said one goes to me, and the other party, and the appellate court.

November 19, 2007 the Ordeal with Turning in Documents for the Case with Venita and the United States Supreme Court

With the problems I faced, I found it compelling to send attorney Melvin Smith papers to stop Venita my former wife from getting my insurance money from the accident. This would be an enormous challenge because there are so many details and incidents to remember. I am talking about over two hundred pages of papers to look up, and provide attorney Smith evidence to win this case. The first thing is where you start when taking on assignments.

Melvin said, "I just want to see you get your money. It was $ 2500 dollars. I can do a lot with that type of money."

I looked through the documents, and took out the relevant ones, and labeled them as exhibits. Venita acted foolish on the day of the rehearing for termination of child support by coming into the cashier's office trying to provoke me into fighting her. I did the best thing to stay out of trouble and ignore her. All I needed for her to do was to get me involved in an incident where I would be charged with assault. I sent Melvin papers which I felt could help in the case. It consisted of a lot of hard work. Correspondence I wanted attorney Smith to get was dropped into his mailbox. Most of the documents were lettered with exhibit numbers. Other items were placed in Venita's folders. Difficulty sat in when trying to meet Melvin's deadline of Friday. With Venita leaving the state, she was not supposed to get no child support whatsoever.

<u>November 27, 2007</u> I went to court on a violation of running a stop sign. The officer stopped me a block from 19th and Cass Avenue as I traveled west on Cass Avenue. On the right side of the street stood the stop sign and I drove a few yards down the street going in a westward direction. All of a sudden I saw a policeman driving down the street in back of me, and he flashed his lights for me to stop.

"Is this your car?" He asked me. I said, "Yes,"

The officer checked to see if I was wearing my seat belt and asked for my insurance papers.

"Do you know why I stopped you?" he said.

I said," I do not know."

"It was because you ran a stop sign. You roared straight passed it."

On 11-27-07, I went to court and pleaded not guilty.

The female judge said, "What do you plead guilty or not guilty?"

I said, "not guilty."

"You are a security officer, and this does not look too good on your record, and plus the police officer has to prove how you ran pass the stop sign. That will be 41 dollars, and you can have two months to pay it off."

Leaving out of the judge's office, I felt good because I was able to standup for my rights. The policemen did not show up for court.

December 28, 2007-Protest Letter and the Story Behind It

Dear Mr. Berg,

My name is Charles Pointer and my race is African American. I have been coming to your copying business for about 15 years after I graduated from Washington University in 1985. I have never experienced any type of discrimination or prejudice behavior from any of your employees until December 28, 2007. I do prose work by representing myself in court, and I came by your store to have nine copies, and an original of an appellate brief, so I could present it to the 22th Missouri Appellate Court. One of your employees who is light skinned but probably mixed with African American blood waited on me. My question to him was could I get one original and nine copies done.

The gentleman said, "This is a legal question and I can not help you."

I said, "Could you get me someone to do the work. I do not want to be bothered with you."

He said, "No I am all you got."

I requested to speak with the manager, but they said he was at lunch.

One African American female came up to the counter, and I told her what I wanted, and she gave me an original and nine copies. She did not say this was a legal problem, and did the job I wanted her to do.

It was difficult trying to staple the briefs, but I asked in a professional manner, if they could get me a stapler to complete my brief. Being five days passed the deadline, I needed the job completed on the day I came to the store. I completed the job, and asked to speak with the manager. When the manager came, I tried to explain to her the clerk treated the white customers better than me, and it was a problem with how to make nine copies of my brief and an original, not a legal problem.

While I spoke to the manager, the gentleman called the police, and there was no need for that. He only wanted to keep from telling the truth. If the female employee who ran copies could do the job, he could have done the same thing too. The male clerk did not let me tell what took place, and lied saying I harassed everyone in the store, and he got to the point where he wanted to fight me.

He kept yelling out loud, "Let's go to the back of the store!"

I was asked to leave the store, and I did because most of the employees were trying to restrain him. I left the store thinking everything was over, and while getting into my car to go home, about eight of your employees came running out of the store trying to restrain this clerk from fighting me. This wild action made me feel humiliated, but I listened to your employees who requested that I get into my car and go home. His attempt was to keep me occupied in the parking lot until the police arrived. I did not attempt to attack this fellow in the store, or in the parking lot. I am a first degree black belt and six time Missouri state champion, and did not want to fight him.

I did go back to the store several times, but I did not see this person in the store again, but this is what I experienced with this store clerk, and saw how a person could hate you just because the color of your skin is black. I did not know this individual, and wanted not to cause him any problems.

March 3, 2008 News from the United States Supreme Court

Today I received a letter from the United States Supreme Court from a Jeffery Akins. After two years of trying to convince the court, I received the Eighth Circuit Appellate Court decision passed the ninety day time limits. I constantly sent correspondence to Ruth Jones, clerk of the court, telling her I never received it after the October 19, 2006 decision. Mr. Akins letter said I had to file a motion with the writ. I did file a motion to file out of time, because I did not get the decision from the appellate court until after the 90 day deadline, to file the brief, to the United States Supreme Court.

April 26, 2008 Constantly Litigating

I have been constantly meeting with Bob Williams at the Julia Davis Library. Bob is a photographer, who fights as an advocate, for people involved in social causes. When I did freelance work for the North Side Journal, he took pictures of the Normandy High School Choir. In parts of this litigation, one argument in my case against Bertha was that she said I never paid any child support, but at a hearing the child support administrator said I paid $ 11,000 dollars in support to her. I felt I met the child support obligation, and anything else I made was mine. I felt the child support people should not get my income tax from me for Venita, because I was not notified to appear in court on March 7, 1990, to take part in the divorce or the custody of my children. The judge gave Venita the large amount of child support without me being in court to say anything about it. I should have been given notice to be in court that day.

May 6, 2008—Arguing My Case in Court against the Energy Assistance Organization

I went and argued my case against the energy assistance organization, and I had a problem trying to decide where to park. I drove over to the church parking lot. I did not think the church members would have my car tolled away. The Old Court House was a few block away, so I walked in a quick pace. My attire consisted of a gray pin stripe suit, black shoes, blue dress shirt and my long afro. I looked at the advocacy book which gave advice on what to do and it helped out a lot. Various techniques were used from the book. I explained how appellee used figures, which were not on the check stubs, submitted as evidence by appellee. The effects of living in a cold house made me cook food with a hot plate, and the food came from can foods containing much sodium which made my blood pressure go up releasing protean from my kidneys. I discussed Judge Wilson not addressing promissory estoppel, and he did not give notice; he would dismiss the case. I argued the case was heard in the wrong court, which was a civil, and criminal court, and not an administrative court. I said after hearing the case; it should have been sent to an appeals commission, and later reviewed by the circuit court, and the court lacked jurisdiction. I sent in an amended answer to a judge. I answered a question which applied to the winter of 6-07 in instead of 07-08. I did not want to commit perjury in this case which was not my intention. Bob Williams said he would come by and take pictures of me going into the court, but he did not make it. I showed where I was a public servant licensed by city and county as a security officer. I felt counsel should not have said Green could not make false statements.

July 4, 2008 Celebrating the 4th of July

Ethel and I went to the festival held in downtown St. Louis for the 4th of July celebration. When coming to downtown St. Louis, it can cause a problem trying to park, but we were able to accomplish this goal. Because of the flooding, the festival was held near Soldiers Memorial. I took pictures of the football Rams cheer leaders, a man juggling long blocks of wood, which were burning, a group of people singing songs, and the thousands of people who attended buying food from the vendors. Later we came home and looked at cable television. The earlier part of the Fourth of July; we spent cooking chicken and ribs and took turns throwing water on the fire, to keep it from burning the food. In the background music sounded good and to past the time away, I did some katas which are a series of movements. I ate much food and did a lot of fun things to occupy our time.

July 5, 2008—More Exciting Activities

While I was at work, I looked at the yellow pages and saw a listing of tourist attractions in the St. Louis area. By reading this section of the book made me want to visit two places which were Fort Bellefontaine and Coca Art Center located in University City on the outskirts of St. Louis. Fort Bell Fontaine was located in a rural area in North St. Louis County, on the side of river banks, of the Missouri River. Ethel and I went to the Coca Art Center, and looked at the art displays, and asked the receptionists for brochures on the activities which took place at their huge facility consisting of beige bricks and large glass windows. I decided to go and drive out to Fort Bellefontaine located on a high hill above the Missouri River. When Lewis and Clark started their journey to explore the Louisiana Purchase, they departed from this fort. By looking at the fort it was built with bricks and steps leading towards the river bank. When coming up the entrance to the fort and children's home, we saw two deer grazing in the grass, but I could not take their pictures because I left my camera at home. We decided to come back and take pictures later on.

On July 18, 2008, I went down to Division 29 and spoke to the clerk. She said she thought a judge's signature was supposed to be on the petition of an Alias Summons. She told me to come to see her on

July 21, and she would tell me what she wanted on the petition and summons. The judge was out of town.

July 27, 2008 More Litigation Efforts

I went down town to Division 29 and turned in my summons and petition, and Judge Hogan did not sign the petition and alias summons because my wife's address was on it. The file clerks in the cashier's office would not let me file the case until the addresses and names were placed on the petition, and Judge Hogan did not speak with me about it.

July 30, 2008

I called the county courts and Pamela who works in the summons department told me to bring documents to them which I wanted with the alias summons. She was nice to talk with and made me feel good. I told her I would come and bring those documents to her.

August 8th, 2008

I got up early and wrote a motion to explain the 28th meeting with Judge Hogan. I turned in another alias summons. This time I wrote me as the petitioner and my social security number the same way as Venita's on the petition. I wrote the Division of Family Service's address on the petition under Venita's.

Melvin Smith was working on a case and I told him to look up the elements of default because the opposing attorney might use that against him. I told him about my case and he told me he could help me if I did something for him. He said he never thought about getting an affirmative defense against the default being used against him. I got denied the petition for reconsideration to send my case to the Missouri Supreme Court.

July 14, 2008

I had a meeting with Rodney and Bob and we did not have the girls at the meeting and Bob's responsibilities at that time was to go to Meachum Park located in Kirkwood, Missouri to investigate the Cookey Thornton case. We will meet with the girls next week.

July 23, 2008 Finding Man's Best Friend My Dog Black

Two weeks ago a black skinny dog was abandoned and left running around in the neighborhood, after the owners who kept him moved, and left him to survive for himself.

This dog's color was black, and he looked awful because of starvation, and you could see his ribs. Mike who lived up the street said he fed him, and I saw pots in front of Miss. Purdue's porch steps containing food and water. Some neighbors tried to feed him, but I placed him in my yard, and kept feeding him, and gave him a permanent home. I called him Black because of his black hair. The previous owners left little room for him to lie down away from his manure. I kept calling the St. Louis Humane Society to come and get him, but they would not take him, because I was not at home to give

Black to them. I did not realize the dog was valuable until I saw him in the back yard chasing after people strolling up and down the alley. When I came home one evening, my next door neighbor said Black was a good watchdog. I kept Black, and fed him, and now he is much bigger and friskier. He eats everything I eat like oatmeal, vegetables, chicken, and his own dog food I buy him. To have fun, I played with Black all the time, and he can catch bread in midair. The neighbor next door owned two dogs, and one of them was a female, and Black liked barking at this dog, and I yelled at him to stop it. I did not want to chain him up to a fence, but Black kept escaping to another yard, and I attempted to get many types of chains to contain him in the backyard, because he broke most of them.

When I am cooking, Black likes to poke his head through the iron bars of my door to see if he can get some table scraps. When I take him on walks, Black enjoys it a lot. I took Black to the veterinarian because he looked as if he could not walk. The animal hospitals were closed on Sunday, which was the day I took him for treatments, but I sat up an appointment that following Monday, so the doctor could see him. It seemed as if every time Black saw a dog he forgot he was sick. Before going to the St. Louis Humane Society, I stopped at the supermarket and got a collar for Black. It was difficult trying to get Black to come out of the house. I tied an electric cord around the new collar I bought him. When we arrived at the hospital, Black could not wait to mess with the other dogs. On the way to the hospital, I put Black on the back seat of my car and lowered my windows and Black looked out the window with his tongue hanging from his mouth. As I drove, Black tried to put his head through the opening between two seats to see what I was doing, and made attempts to come up front to the driver's side of the car but I kept him from doing it. I drove much slower to keep from hitting the other cars. For some reason or another, Black enjoyed riding in my car. One of the drivers kept waving at Black as he looked at them through the window. When I came to a stop, Black crashed into the floor. The clerk told me it would be $ 50 dollars to bring Black in for treatment. I explained to the attendant what was wrong with him such as him limping when he walked, and seemed lifeless, as though he did not want to walk or bark. The attendant gave Black some treats to eat which he seemed to enjoy. They placed a muzzle on Black's nose to keep him from biting the attendant who weighed Black and took his temperature.

"What seems to be the problem?" the attendant said.

"I think he ate something in the backyard," I said. "My friend Mike said, "I always see Black eating some bark and, weeds, and he probably ate something that poisoned his system."

That might be a possibility I said to myself because Black loves to chew on grass, and, bark from the trees, or lay in the grass, after I always cut it with my lawn mower. I said hello to the doctor and she said, "It seems as if he has a skin problem. What have you been giving him?"

I said, "I gave him some medicine for his rash on his forearms which looked like an infection and some penicillin."

I said, "The rash looked like it was coming off when I applied the cream to the affected area on his body."

She said, "Stop giving him any medication or creams, I will give him some pills to take which can help him." I gave him a skin graft which came up negative. I gave him some other tests in which the results will come back in two or three weeks, but as of now the skin grafts were negative."

I said thank you to the attendant and the nurse.

As I made arrangements to make payments for Black I said to the clerk, "Black has always looked out for me and keeps people out of the backyard. No one has broken into my house since Black was put in the backyard, and when I placed the steel doors, and metal window bars, on my basement windows. Black took care of me so I have to look out for him to make sure he gets the best treatment."

When feeding Black, I placed his medication on some bread with mayonnaise on it. Black was so eager to eat that he did not notice the medication in the sandwich spread. Earlier, before I took him to the hospital, I noticed Black was not in the basement area. Curiosity filled my mind and I wondered if Black went into another room to die? Sounds echoed out of the room like there was some life in it, and to my surprise, it was Black sleeping on a bed spread. One thing I noticed about Black was he did not like sleeping on anything that was hard like a concrete floor. Sleeping on a concrete floor is something Black avoids all the time and looks for something soft to sleep on. When Black stopped barking, I knew something was wrong, and took him to the doctor. Now Black does not appear too sick since I have been giving him his medication. One hundred and fifty dollars was worth spending to keep Black alive. Black has been a great source of companionship and joy. The vet told me not to use any medications on Black. I spoke with Ethel and she said I might be giving him the wrong type of dog food.

Ethel said, "Charles my friend said she fed her dog food from Aldi and it made him sick."

I took her advice and fed Black dog food made by Ralston Purina, and gave him a bath, and washed him down with hydrogen peroxide, and he felt much better as a result of the changes and his health improved.

October 2008

Trying to get Bertha served was a problem. The sheriff's department took summons out to her house but they could not ever catch her. I tried to get the library officials to set up a time when she could be subpoenaed but they would not cooperate with me. Several people at the library lied when they said they would speak with people in personnel to see if something could be done about it. I later found out that Bertha worked at the Lewis and Clark Library.

With Vernita there was a scheduled meeting for the 18th of September but on September 14th hurricane Ike came and knocked down the telephone wires preventing a telephone hearing from taking place. I mailed the bottom part of the notice of child support to Jefferson

City asking for a rehearing. I received a call from the rehearing office division that I needed a rehearing. Lisa who was located in Jefferson City said she would notify the hearing office division that I needed a rehearing. I received a call from the rehearing office saying I needed to get verification from the telephone company explaining a repairman came out to my house to fix the telephone. I called AT and T and the call office in Chicago and they could not send out that type of information. I spoke to an African American, and she did not give me the corporate office number so I could call them, and explain that I needed something in writing stating the repairman came out to fix my phone, therefore, I could not have any hearing whatsoever. She tried to help me by calling the corporate office, and said he would call me at work, but I never received a telephone call concerning it. I spoke to Bob and he said he would speak with me on Thursday at the Julia Davis Library about the matter. Bob said some of the same things happened to him too. I spoke to the repairman and he gave me the repair number and his name was Mike.

November 4, 2008 the Presidential Election and the Election of Our First African American President of the United States

This was a spectacular history making night when Barrack Obama became elected the first African American president of the United States. John McCain started out winning the smaller states in the South, but Barrack won the major industrial states in the North and many more in the South, Midwest, California, Washington, and New Mexico. I looked at the Allen DE generous show and many people attending it cheered for Barrack Obama. Children's groups singed some songs on her show. Comedians made jokes saying Obama had nothing on him to make jokes about. I looked at the television and news casters talked about the election. They said 50% of the popular vote went to Barrack Obama and both houses of congress increased with Democrats. Ethel and I watched the election results on television and were thrilled to see Obama the first African American elected president of the United States. I voted for the Obama Biden ticket and my good friend Robert was in front of me registering to vote. My neighbor Tina stood in line registering to vote too. I voted a straight Democratic ticket with their candidates. I voted against the judges who gave me a hard time in court. The janitorial workers on the job were very happy about Obama winning the election and as I drove to work I could hear gun shots being fired into the air.

September 28, 2008 My Good Friend Tom

This unique fellow by the name of Tom comes to physical therapy with his wife who works there. In front of my desk are some lounge chairs and this is where Tom and I talked about civic events of the day, such as the presidential debates between McCain and Senator Barrack Obama, the economy, the war in Irag, his upbringing, and my early life history up to now. There were things we had in common such as the reasons for going to college during the Vietnam War, and I said to him, "Tom I did not want to fight in this war. Every evening at 6 p.m., I watched the evening news, and saw soldiers shooting at the Vietcong, and did not feel it was justified to fight in this international conflict."

I told him I decided I did not want to fight in this war to die for this country.

"Charles I went to college for some of the same reasons."

The city of Chicago, Illinois is where Tom grew up at, and I remember him saying, "Charles I did not grow up with a sliver spoon in my pocket. I worked hard for what I wanted and obtained in my life."

We both were born in the same year, 1950. We enjoyed practicing karate as a common sport for both of us. When discussing inventors, George Washington Carver was admired by him and me also. Tom's sense of humor was interesting because he loved people of different races, and many of his friends were African American. Getting a college education was something me and Tom shared with each other, and he earned a degree in agriculture.

I looked forward to talking with Tom because he is a Republican, and I a Democrat, and love to debate about different topics, and he will always be remembered.

October 30, 2008

I went to Division 29 where Judge Hogan presided and gave the clerk my petition and summons, and asked her to take it to Judge Hogan. The clerk came back and said my case was dismissed.

I said "This is a mistake because the case was dismissed without prejudice and given a new case number. She went back and told the judge, and the clerk came back and said, Judge Hogan said to file the petition on the third floor in the filing room. I was elated because the court clerks on the first floor said the headings were not correct, and I should have included Venita's address in the headings. Judge Hogan disagreed, and rejected the summons, and petition. I attended two settlement conferences, and she told me to get a lawyer, and I told her I was a paralegal. I spoke to Sherry, and she suggested that I look at some files done by lawyers on child support, and see how they are written. I went to the filing office, and they let me see a document filed by child support officials. I noticed they used the social security numbers of the parties. The end result was her excepting the changes, plus I amended the petition showing the changes I made. That same day I went out to the Clayton courts in the county and filed my other petition in the circuit court. I paid the summons fee and she noticed I had the wrong case number on it. I later changed it on all the motions. Instead of having Bertha served at her home, they served her at the Lewis and Clark Library where she worked. Leaving the court, I felt happy and I made sure I paid the fee, and they said they would see if the judge would allow me to add another party which was the Division of Family Services of Missouri.

Tuesday November 25, 2008

Called Division 29 and they said I did not pay the $ 30 dollar fee to have child support officials served. The clerk down stirs said I did not have to pay their sheriff because the interstate people in Jefferson City had to be served. I went upstairs and I told them Steve told me to wait until I heard from Judge Hogan but nothing took place. After waiting, I called Division 29, and the clerk, who was an African American female, said Steve did not know I had not paid the fee. The clerk down stirs said I did not have to pay the St. Louis City Sherriff's Department. I went back to Division 29 and she went over to the clerk in the division across from her. Earlier a clerk from downtown went up to division 29, but the clerk was not there. I waited until she came from lunch at 1:30.While I waited downstairs, I spoke with Bruce who shined shoes in the basement. He said Judge Grady helped him get a job shining people's shoes. The clerk who came over helped the clerk in Division 29 and told me to leave two petitions with her and said the summons and papers would be sent to me.

On December 3, 2008, I called the summons department and Benica said Division 29 sent my folder down to them with the petition and alias summons. My buy out vacation days was turned in. The badge showing the time of my license renewal was turned in. The date of my license was December 23, 2008.

January 9, 2009

Reverend Stevens went to court to turn in the amended petition, and when he appeared in court, he was told the case was closed, and the decision was made on June 2, but he did not have notice of this. The court wanted him to get a court DE novo, and pay $45 dollars filing fee, and post a $ 1000 dollars filing fee and $ 1000 dollar bond.

I spoke to Sherry and she said respondent was in default judgment for serving Mr. Stevens improperly, and he should apply for a motion to set aside the judgment, because he was not served. The process server placed the petition in Mr. Steven's mailbox.

On January 12, 2009,

I did so many things and at first I ate and fed Black who is my dog and gathered up all of my papers to take to court. I am fighting the traffic people for placing a ticket on my car. There were no signs on the vacant lot telling people who owned the land, or no directions on what to do, or rules governing parking procedures. I felt it was time to protest. Parking meters were on both sides of the curb facing some cars. There were no meters on the vacant parking lot. St. Louis University police said they did not know who owned the land and I did not either. I went to the employment office and faxed the papers to the ticket bureau requesting a hearing on the matter. After that I went out to the court house located in Clayton, Missouri, and filed my response to attorney's counter claim. I went to the law library and one of the law professors helped me find Rule 44b Enlargement and how a person could file out of time and have the court keep jurisdiction. I found other case law on people filing out of time, and still the judge granted them time to execute, and finish their petitions, and file them also. Using the copying machine; I was able to do all of my copying at their building.

January 16, 2009

I went to Division 29 and Judge Hogan did not seem too happy to speak with me. The judge spoke to the other lawyers with respect. I called the judge only to see if I had the Division of Family Services and Venita Washington served. He just flicked through the pages of the file and asked questions knowing I did not have the same documents. I explained that the Boulder County sheriffs sent me back summons papers because Venita moved from her old address and could not be served. The sheriff in Cole County had not written me back yet and I felt Pro-Se should be treated much better. Judge Grady ordered Judge Hogan's secretaries to prepare my alias summons. The judge said he would dismiss my case if Venita was not served.

January 19, 2009

I sit at my desk onDr. Martin Luther King's birthday. Many people are attending the activities and tomorrow Barrack Obama will be sworn in the as president of the United States of America. I have to go to the courtroom located in Clayton, Missouri tomorrow because I set up a hearing. Attorney Buckingham and I talked to each other, and she said she got an extension up to January 28th to answer my petition, but I'll go anyway to show I kept my appointment. I wrote a rough draft of my letter to Judge Dowd to request that one of their judge's show more respect to Pro-Se litigants. Much prejudice is shown towards Pro-Se people.

January 20, 2009

I went to court in St. Louis County to see if the hearing would take place so that respondent would answer my petition and summons at first. The lawyer appointed to answer my petition went on family leave. I filed a default judgment because it was passed the thirty days to respond but on the morning I filed it the opposing side came and asked for a continuance up to January 28th. I felt that since I called up the hearing I should be there. The clerk said the hearing would be on Thursday at 8:45. I think I might survive because I used 44b and requested five more days to turn in the petition due to excusable neglect.

January 21, 2009

When arguing this case against the Division of Family Service which dealt with the denial of energy assistance, the basic problem was that the appellate court said they could not challenge the decision of trial court under Judge Wilson, but only the decision of the administrative hearing judge. Judge Wilson said he would stay the case and give both sides his answer, but he dismissed the case instead. I argued Judge

Wilson should have warned both parties that he was going to do this because he treated his untimely action as a motion for summary judgment. At the hearing all the people had documents except Judge Wilson. Miss. Green misrepresented the facts, and gave no summary of how she got those figures from a foundation in a policy book. The most disappointing thing about this is the appellate court said they could not correct trial court error, and their role was not to criticize appellant's brief. They said I should have placed the cases I used in the brief instead of at the end of it. The word reversible error they said was used too much. I found case law which said the appellate court could not measure the weight of the evidence against appellant. It was brought to the Missouri Supreme Court, but I filed out of time because the law library was closed, and I could not complete the brief because the statute of limitations may have run out. I got involved in so many cases it might be too late.

January 21, 2009 Pointer v Pointer

Petitioner made the mistake of filing a temporary injunction instead of a permanent one. I'll have to study the document again to write a better explanation of all accounts of what took placed. I explained how I lived in a cold house because my ex-wives were taking my money. This was a time when I did not have any paralegal courses in law. The tide changed when I took over thirty hours in paralegal law courses taught by attornies.

January 22, 2009

I have to face attorney Appleton who is saying I lacked subject matter jurisdiction because I filed out of time which was incorrect but I used Rule 44 In largement and to justify it, I wrote a twelve page response.

Jan 23, 2009

I appeared in Division 18 under Judge Sirhanahand and he said subject matter jurisdiction was at stake because the memo I presented did not have the right division number on it and the clerk said I did not bring it up for a hearing. Attorneys Appleton and Buckingham were there too. The judge said he would look into the file and see who sent the memo. I requested three more days to turn in my summons and petition on the 26th, 2008 but only March 31st was recorded by the court. Judge Sirhanahand said the other attorneys asked for more days. In the federal court I just put things in the basket and thought it would be sent to the division. I am thinking about withdrawing without prejudice and refilling it again. I could settle it but the issues I want to bring to the court are very dear to me. If a person is already paying support how can an agency take money from him when there is no law saying this can happen. They have many laws with liens on various items but no law governing them.

Sunday January 25th, 2009

Appearing in court on January 22th with attorney Buckingham and Appleton, I showed Judge Sirhanahan the memo showing I requested for five more days and my opponent asked for 60 days. They were in default judgment and the judge said he would check and see what happened to the request. The clerk got it and filed it instead of giving it to someone who could give me permission for more days. I was told to take the case to a court which had jurisdiction and I found case law which said the decisions of a court lacking jurisdiction is void.

January 28, 2009

I went to traffic court to appeal a decision. The officer who gave me a ticket was not there and the law said you must be able to confront your accusers. I showed the fellow who acted as judge and jury the pictures where cars were parked on Spring Avenue and cars on the vacant lot. There were no signs showing who owned the land, or any directions given as to who could park on it. The city officials said there were too many unincorporated properties in the city to put warning signs on them. I told him I would file a petition in the circuit court. When I found out it would be $170 dollars to file the petition, I decided not to fight over a $25 dollar ticket. I might alert the mayor and the news media about this. Ten years later I paid $ 75 dollars to end this matter.

I went to the court of the 22th district to see when the Division of Family Service was served their summons and petition, but it was not in the system when Mr. Hodgson checked. I spoke to Miss. Carpenter and she said to give the court a copy of the letter. The Boulder County sheriff sent me a reply saying Venita moved from her address on Kimbach in Longmont, Colorado. I stopped by attorney Marsh's office and checked on my food poisoning case. He said the other side did not settle because the hospital was not sure of what caused the upset stomach, but he said a new manager might take over and settle with us, and it was a matter of waiting to see what they would like to do. We talked about the case with Venita Washington who took my kids to Colorado. The attorney representing the other side said they wanted more days to answer my petition. Actually they were in default judgment but attorney Marsh said not to challenge it because judges are normally lenient in giving extra days to file answers to petitions.

January 29, 2009 Why Sue the Division of Family Services

The principle reason I am suing the division of family services is because they are taking money from people who are already paying child support that is ordered from the court. This is stealing and there is no law that says the state can take your money when you are already paying support. I speak to many people who pay support and other income is taken from them. The money must be certified as to what is taken and what amount goes to the non-custodial parent who is paying it. I faced much bias being Pro-Se. It appeared some of the judges did not like dealing with Pro-Se litigants, and I reminded Judge Stelzer I had Sixth Amendment rights to represent myself. Many times I called Sherry who is a Pro-Se, and represents herself in court and, goes through the same things I experience as a Pro-Se. On this day of the 29th, I'll probably reply to attorney Buckingham's response to my petition.

February 2, 2009

I went to court located in Clayton, Missouri and I wrote a response to attorney Buckingham's reply to my summons. I was able to site some things which were incorrect. I saw where attorney Buckingham said I did not send any pleadings until December 3, 2008. I produced at least 15 documents showing they were court stamped before December 3, 2008. I showed where discrimination took place when everyone at the hearing had packets except me which was disparate treatment and violation of my 14th Amendment rights.

February 18, 2009

On February 16, 2009 I, Charles Pointer filed for a continuance to the Missouri Court of Appeals based on Judge Surhanohand saying I filed a motion for a new trial which was not true. Pointer only filed a notice of appeal but trial court tried to confuse the issues. Trial court said there was nothing in his decision showing any errors. I said only the appellate court has jurisdiction to determine error in actions committed by trial court. Trial court did not provide a Missouri statute indicating what format should be placed in a notice of appeal to say petitioner filed it incorrectly. I explained I could not pay the filing fee, and my appeal should not be stopped by trial court. I indicated the right to appeal should have been forwarded to the appellate court. I spoke to Charlie about it and showed him where the judge said I requested a new trial which was not true. I hope the honorable appellate court will look at all of the contents of my notice of appeal, and give me this precious right protected by the constitution of the United States of America. I explained how trial court showed favoritism with the issue of excusable neglect. I felt if the clerks could send information by the various attorneys, they could send my request to the proper judge, who could give me the requested days. I did not file my request out of time. It was filed as a continuance on the due date, and trial court used cases where defendants filed one day late. This was not done by petitioner. Clerks should have forwarded petitioner's request to a judge who could grant those days. Trial court said he did not see Division 18 on the request. Division 18 would not be on the request because it was not being filed at that time. After it was filed, Division 18 was placed on it. I said attorney Buckingham did not come to my hearing to discuss the default judgment on January 20, 2009 to discuss why attorney Meyers did not answer my petition after 30 days, and trial court gave them thirty more days to answer. I requested five days using Excusable Neglect Rule 44, but he dismissed my case saying he lacked subject matter jurisdiction, and dismissed the case with prejudice which I felt was unlawful trying to keep me from filing it in trial court again, or to appeal it to the appellate court. Petitioner indicated there were no signs around the tray telling him to take his request to a judge to get it looked at. The clerk should have sent my request to a judge who would respond after seeing it.

All the information was sent to the appellate court for a response. I wrote a letter to Judge Dowd asking him to make judge Stelzer show more respect when speaking to me because he showed it when speaking to other attorneys. I explained how Judge Grady ok'd my alias summons after Judge Hogan would not sign it. The letter indicated my rights to represent myself were guaranteed by the Sixth Amendment, and he tried to control what I could say and how many times I could say it. Not seeing my kids were emphasized too and I had six degrees with one in paralegal studies and criminal justice. I wrote I was denied cert in the United States Supreme Court and did oral argument in the 22th Missouri Appellate Court. Tomorrow, I will file my petitions in the federal court because Mrs. Early kept me from sending my letters to the board of trustees.

A Letter to Judge Dowd

My name is Charles Pointer, and I am requesting that Judge Stelzer treat me with more respect, and speak to me in a tone of voice just like he spoke to other attorneys. When he saw I was African American, and a Pro-Se his whole attitude changed into a bias ugly one. I experienced the same thing with Judge Hogan when she refused to speak with me when I came to two settlement conferences, and Venita and the

Division of Family Services never showed up, and she sent orders to them telling them to come. I saw the presiding judge who was Judge Grady, and he made the court clerks sign my alias summons to have the Division of Family Services and Venita served because Judge Hogan kept telling me to get a lawyer. Before Judge Hogan went to another division an order came from him telling me and the Division of Family Services to come to a settlement conference hearing on January 16, 2009. I came to two such settlements conferences, and the other parties never showed up. Judge Stelzer did not read my petition and skimmed through the folder asking questions. I informed him the sheriff sent back a message they could not serve Venita because she moved to another address.

I had not heard from the sheriff located in Cole County who was supposed to serve The Missouri Division of Family Services. Judge Stelzer tried to stop me from talking, and kept reminding me of how many times I was saying things, as if I could not talk anymore. This is interfering with my First Amendment rights. I reminded him I had Sixth Amendment rights to represent myself after he told me to get myself a lawyer. He just seemed to dislike the Pro-Se petitioner because he spoke to the two white attorneys with more respect, and responded to me like I was a slave, which I did not like. I am requesting that you speak with him about showing more respect when talking with Pro-Se litigants. He's giving a message he does not like Pro-Se litigants. I have six degrees with one in criminal justice, University of Missouri, St. Louis, and an Associate of Art degree in paralegal studies, and have been doing prose work in the federal court for eight years, on the appellate levels leading to being denied cert in the United States Supreme Court. I did oral argument in the 22nd Missouri Appellant Court two times.

Notice of Appeal

Comes Now Charles Henry Pointer to request a Notice of Hearing for the following reasons:

1. Petitioner requested five more days on the due date of his petition which was March 26, 2008 because of excusable neglect. The date petitioner turned in his petition and summons was on March 31, 2008. The court said March 28, 2008.

2. Petitioner sent his papers to attorney Melvin Smith who he said he would handle it as a personal injury case. About three days before the due date, attorney Smith's secretary called and told petitioner to come and get his papers which left him no time to properly do research and file a response on time.

3. Petitioner wrote out a request on the due date requesting five more days on the date the petition and summons was due. The request was done on March 26, 2008 and placed in the basket. There were no signs telling him to take it to a judge

4. Petitioner thought the clerks would deliver this request to the proper judges who would inform him on if he could get the five days to file his petition and summons.

5. The clerks filed the request without doing what was requested of them. If other petitions are sent to the other divisions as requested, my memo should have been sent also.

6. There were no signs saying if you wanted a request done by the court you had to take it up to the judge. If a notice would been placed near the basket where you placed petitions and summons, and other court correspondence saying you had to do this to get a request for my five more days; I would have done it. No Missouri statute was shown to me saying you had to take it to the judge to get something like this done.

7. On the first floor before going upstairs to the courts there are notices posted when changes are being made in the court procedures. Notices should be placed near those baskets telling people they have to take requests up to the judges instead of them thinking if they place such requests in the basket they would be sent to the court officials who could handle them.

8. Trial court said there was no division number 18 going to his court on petitioner's request. There would be no

division number on it because the request was filed on the March 26, 2008 and officially filed on March 31, 2008.

9. Trial court allowed attorney Buckingham 30 more days after attorney Meyers the first assistant attorney was in default and she requested thirty more days on January 28, 2009 to respond and it was granted.

10. Petitioner requested that attorney Buckingham come to a hearing to respond to Petitioner's petition on January 20, 2009 but she never showed up but came to a hearing on January 22, 2009 with attorney Appleton representing Bertha Pointer, and she represented The Division of Family Services.

11. Trial court met with attorney Buckingham when she was in default judgment without her bringing this up for a hearing with petitioner present. A hearing must be scheduled with Petitioner and respondent being present for petitioner to offer rebuttal because she was in default judgment at the time. Trial court allowed attorney Buckingham to not come to the requested hearing for default judgment. When petitioner arrived on the hearing date, trial court secretary said she was granted more time. Respondent was allowed to use excusable neglect when attorney Meyers was in default judgment and granted thirty more days by trial court which totaled sixty days but refused to take into consideration attorney Melvin Smith pulled out of the

case giving petitioner little time to turn in his petition and summons on the due date. Petitioner cannot help it if a basket is assigned to put requests in and the clerk does not look at what the request is asking and immediately do not get someone to take that request to the proper judge, who could carry it out. Petitioner did not have a division to send his request to because it was not filed yet. Trial court used discretion in granting attorney Buckingham thirty more days when attorney Meyers was in default because of family leave but did not use discretion when petitioner never could not properly execute his case due to excusable neglect because attorney Melvin Smith and a clerk who did not take the petition request to a judge who could answer his request for five more days. Petitioner requested five more days with the judge's discretion using Rule 44b. If trial court was lenient in granting DFS everything she wanted, the same courtesy should have been granted to petitioner. Attorney Smith's number was listed in the request and trial court could have called him to hear his side of the story in his ability to use discretion using Rule 44 B1 Time and Enlargement. That rule did not say you could go directly to a judge and ask for more time. As the United States Supreme Court justice Thurgood Marshall said, "Equal is Equal." Trial court lacked subject matter jurisdiction to dismiss petitioner's case with prejudice to keep him from refilling it again in the state court. This was showing bias against petitioner.

April 3, 2009

I filed a civil suit against Venita Washington because the state intercepted my stimulus money, federal tax refunds, and state taxes. At the hearing Mr. Zumwalt did not talk about the money which was owed me after the child support was taken out. Venita was not at the meeting which I felt violated my civil rights. At the October telephone hearing she was present, but now she did not take part, and Miss. Breummer represented Venita. For about three weeks, I did research on federal and state intercepts of money from back child support. In the research, it said that hearings must be given and the money taken must be certified.

None of those things took place. I used case law showing where a father was already up to date on his back support and did not owe this support. Other research said that offsets must be taken when a person's behind in back support payments by three months for federal and state offsets to be taken. None of this was spoken about at the hearing. I went to the circuit court to file it because you have thirty days to do it.

April 12, 2009

I have just completed the jurisdictional statement for my appellate brief. I did the statement of the case two days ago. I corrected the letters

I sent to the attorney general. I guess I was too cold to catch that error. First thing in the morning I will send a letter back with the corrections on it. I've spent a lot of time going to the Julia Davis Library using their internet to look up cases for my brief. For the en banc case, I must look up cases on jurisdiction.

When going to court in downtown St. Louis, I walked over the bridge and watched the trains go back and forth. I filled out the cover sheet and went to Division 1 to get Judge Dowd to sign a form for In Forma Pauperis. The judge asked me why my debt was so close to the assets. I left off the $ 22,000 dollars I was paying on a school loan. After he signed it, I left the courthouse feeling very good. I used cases where the man was in full compliance with his child support, and his federal tax money should not have been taken when filing it. The biggest problem was making sure I could file the petition on time so the court would have jurisdiction over the case. Doing the work exhausted me, but I proofread my petition for errors. Trying to get to the circuit court can be a problem because from 3:30 p.m. to 6 p.m. you cannot park downtown. Before going to court, I stopped at the employment office and made copies. Deciding to park across the bridge, I did not have to worry about getting a ticket at the meters near the courthouse. The weather was good as I walked across the bridge, and stopped to look at the trains traveling under it, going in different destinations. I held my hat in my hands to keep the wind from blowing my hat off my head.

April 15, 2009

Bernard, Raymond, and I were at McDonalds Restaurant on Natural Bridge and Kings Highway, and something very humorous took place with my friend by the name of Raymond. Raymond, Bernard, and I go up to the restaurant and eat breakfast. Most of the time I come after I work from 11.p.m to 7:a.m. which is the graveyard shift. This particular morning Raymond was dressed in his Catholic white collar priest shirt complete with a suit. About two years ago, Raymond came up to the restaurant wearing three or four shirts. Most of the time, Raymond did not have any money and asked for a loan from the people who came there to eat. Sometimes I gave Raymond a couple of dollars to buy some coffee if I thought he needed it. No one knew where Raymond lived and he never told us. A lot of fellows came to the restaurant and most of the time the great issues of the world got debated on which made the manager angry, and hollowed at us to the point of wanting to put us out. One time on this day Stan came in and asked Raymond to give him a dollar and Raymond refused and I asked him to give Stan one of the dollars he owed me. Again Raymond kept talking real loud, and making different gestures about the thoughts on his mind at that time. I said, "Raymond you're wearing the cloth of a Catholic priest. You should show that Christian love and give the brother a dollar."

Bernard and I kept on laughing because Raymond likes to give advice on a lot of things and he was like a guru to us. Raymond dropped his income tax refund showing his real name, and that he lived in a hotel on Olive Avenue. Raymond told us the reason he looked so dirty was because he lived with a women who took a lot of his money, but he left her and got his own place, and now he dressed much better. He is a wonderful person and before my book was published he gave me much support when the other fellows felt I was lying about my book, "The Making of a Black Belt Karate Champion" which was published in the month of March, 2012.

April-09 Follow Up At McDonalds

At this restaurant I met many interesting people who were great conservationists. This restaurant was located on Natural Bridge on the city's north side. For years, I came up there to eat. I remember speaking with Raymond, an African American who could talk you to death about anything. When Raymond started talking, you could not make him stop. At any moment the other fellows challenged him and Raymond found a way to avoid answering the critical questions, and loved to talk about the ups and downs, in a man and women relationship. This type of behavior made enemies of the manager who threaten to put us out. Everyday Raymond rode to the restaurant on his bike and sometimes he brought all of his clothes with him. Sometimes he wore two or three pairs of pants and about four or five shirts to keep warm.

April 19, 2009

I spoke with Sherry. I worked on the argument section of the brief which would be presented on April 22, 2009. I have doubled spaced the, lines and did some revisions, which I liked. I narrowed my issues down to three points which are jurisdiction, due process, and misrepresentation, and denial of my First and Fourth Amendment rights. I went to the law library at Washington University and St. Louis University to research for case law.

May 9, 2009

I filed my small claims suit to get $ 300 dollar from the Navy Federal Credit Union Foundation. I spoke to Kelyan and told him I was going to file it. I called the secretary of state's office in Virginia and the clerk told me the registered agent for the credit union was Thomas Connelly. The first statement from the Naval Federal Credit Union was that they could not tell if the money order was altered but it had white out on it showing my name and address was erased with whiteout. A friend of mine said I should rewrite the petition and ask for more money but I changed my award because I spent $ 90 dollars to have it filed. She wanted me to add Laclede Gas on as a party, but I disagreed because it was not proven Laclede Gas employees had anything to do with getting my money order. There was proof my money order was cashed in Virginia. This was the principal place to sue. I could not assume that Laclede Gas officials took the check. The clerk at the small claims office made copies of everything, and sent the petition, and summons to the Naval Federal Credit Foundation in Vienna, Virginia.

On May 9, 2009, I went to see my former professor, and gave her a large amount of money to start my case, because I got tire of paying out my money to child support and never seeing my kids. I cannot call or write them. I set for a small interview and explained she could use the law which said when the noncustodial parent is kept from seeing the kids; he can get a rebate for it. I spoke with attorney Jarmin, and she is going to have Venita served by publication, and she is drawing up papers for a petition. Venita had to answer the notice in 45 days starting with April 18, 2009 to sometime in June, and Venita has not, responded as of yet.

On May 12, 2009, I spoke to the Cole County Sheriff, and they served the Division of Family Services on April 29, 2009. They have not responded as of yet. The problem as I see it is that Venita has done so much wrong that it's like a trail has been created which will make it hard to defend. Venita doesn't want people to know where she is staying at which means she can be found in default. I sued the Division of Family Service for some money because they did not have Venita to take part in the hearing. This denies me of my due process rights to confront my accusers. The social worker had no right in my opinion to represent Venita and the man has to pay to get an attorney to represent himself. I might have to take the case to federal court because of du-process rights to a fair hearing. My back support is going to Venita and she should have been made to appear at the hearing so all parties to the litigation would be heard.

May 31, 2009

I amended the petition to say I filed my petition on time April 3, 2009. The department of social service gave Venita money on April 16, 2009. The child support organization was served on April 29, 2009. They were supposed to respond by May 29, 2009. I spoke to Sherry and she said to wait to see if they responded on it before filing my default judgment. I did file an amended petition because they gave Venita the income tax money before the matter was presented to the court. Judge Stelzer saw where Venita and the people representing her were served on May 29, 2009 and I set up the motion for June 7, 2009. Judge Stelzer said they did not have time to respond but I felt he should have declared them in default. He set June 26, at 9:30 for them to appear in court.

July 4, 2009

It's been raining since 6 p.m. after I left Ethel's house. I stopped and fed my dog Black. Miss. Jarmin handled my two cases against Venita and the Missouri Division of Family Services. I filed my petition on April 3, 2009 and they gave Venita the money on April 16, 2009 before the matter came before the court. I appeared in Judge Stelzer's court on June 4th with a default judgment because the Division of Family Services was served on April 29, 2009. Judge Stelzer said he would have court on June 26, 2009 with all the parties present, but he was supposed to rule in my favor because you do not have to give notice when the other side is in default. I later received a letter from Judge Stelzer.

July 27, 2009

I went to traffic court and I was going to address the issues, but the judge said he wanted to dismiss the other ticket. I felt it was important to pay the first ticket and have it over with. I later took Kelyan out to Big Bend where there are nothing but camera lights out there. I got frustrated because paying the fines kept me from getting some things I wanted to buy like tile for my floors. I'll have to look for a higher paying job.

July 28, 2009

I appeared with my lawyer attorney Jarman to file a default judgment against Venita and the Division of Family Services. Before coming to court, I called her on July 28, 2009. I got up on that morning and did my usual cleanup of my body and ironed my white shirt and put on a suit. When I started towards McDonalds Hamburgers, I wondered if I had unplugged the iron and decided to go back home to see. Driving as fast as I could; I arrived at home, and checked to see if I took the ironing wire plug out of the electrical socket, located on the wall in my kitchen. Seeing that the ironing plug was not in the wall, I headed towards the court located on 12th and Tucker. Not having any breakfast, I stopped and got me some biscuits and gravy. Reaching my destination, I went to Division 31 in Judge Sweeny's courtroom.

Waiting and sitting on the bench was attorney Jarman, and she said, "Hello," and I sat down.

Judge Sweeny was handling other cases which came before him.

"Charles come outside. I want to talk to you," Jarman said, "Were the Division of Family Services served and Venita served ?"

I said, "Yes." And showed her correspondence where Sheriff Dinkins served them. I showed where the Division of Family Services and the Boulder County Sheriff were served. When we got in front of the Judge Sweeny he said," Mr. Pointer you are representing yourself?"

I did not say anything and attorney Jarman said, "I am representing Charles."

Judge Sweeny said," Charles the other side is requesting an extension to August 21, 2009 and we will get in touch with you."

Attorney Jarmin noticed that in the pleadings attorney Buckingham requested more time to reply on the August 21, hearing but did not realize she requested an extension and promised to answer my petition on July 27, 2009. As of July 28, 2009 they have not responded as of yet.

Attorney Jarmin said, "They are relying on the August date to request 30 more days to respond, if they do not respond by the end of the week I'll file for a default judgment. I decided to carefully look at the mailbox to make sure, and hoped they would not send a response to me to file a default judgment.

The United States District Federal Court 8th Circuit

Notice of Appeal

I am appealing the following section of the trial court's decision:

1. Trial court is using the en banc order showing prejudice which outweighs its probative value.

2. All of the cases I filed resulted in summary judgment, failure to state a claim, or resjudicata, and some were settled which other lawyers get, when litigating their cases. All the district judges did not sign the en banc order.

Plaintiff is challenging the following: The complaint alleges that officials at Washington University School of Law did not respond to his letters regarding his several attempts to gain admission to the law school.

Response: In this case No:05 MC658 RSW plaintiff did not write letters to the admissions committee of the law school for comments as to why he was not given a non-discriminatory reason for being rejected from the law school. Plaintiff wrote letters to members of the Board of Trustees at Washington University and Ida Early secretary to the Board of Trustees opened the letters and did not forward them to board members.

Plaintiff is challenging the following: The complaint is frivolous and it is similar to previous complaints brought against St. Louis University School of Law. See Pointer v. St. Louis University Law School 4:01cv1467 TCM (ED)

Response: Those two cases are not similar to this case <u>No 4: 05 MC 658 RWS</u> Plaintiff did not write letters to the Board of Trustees at St. Louis University, and trial court has not produced any letters showing he wrote the Board of Trustee members at St. Louis University. Plaintiff wrote letters to the board of trustees at Washington University. Three of the cases were settled by me and the other attorneys.

Plaintiff is challenging the following:

It is ordered that plaintiff's motion to file a civil action is denied. A petition for relief is void.

3   None of the other parties to any of the suits filed charges against me saying I filed malicious litigation against them.

4   Its unconstitutional for a judge to use personal bias to get permission from them to file a petition in court because I am filing in forma pauperis or paying a filing fee. This must be applied to all attorneys. No unconstitutional amendment is being used to support his actions.

5   Trial court has not identified any case in his court order showing frivolous law suits filed by plaintiff.

6   Trial court lied when he said plaintiff filed this case against officials because they did not respond to his requests sent to them. This case is about Ida Early secretary to the board of trustee's members and refusing to send my letters to the trustees because she did not like the contents of the letters. No search warrant was used to open his mail and there was

no probable cause to do this. The mail was considered first class and not subject to inspection.

7   Trial court used two cases in his decision which were irrelevant which did not deal with the issues pertaining to my First and Fourth Amendment rights. Plaintiff could not utilize all of his administrative remedies to speak with law school officials and board of trustee members to mediate and discuss the issues.

8   Judge Sipple got all of plaintiff's petitions against the law school. Why is it he got all of plaintiff's petitions in his attempts to keep me from bringing my cases to the court? He did not have the other party served.

9   Trial court did not give a reason for the following procedure: As a result plaintiff's motion to file a new civil action will be denied.

Trial court has not given a reason for denying me of my constitutional rights to file a new action.

It is hereby ordered that plaintiff's motion for leave of court to file a civil action is denied. There are no reasons for this unlawful action to deny plaintiff of his civil rights. Judge Sipple is denying my right to a trial of my peers without any explanation. He has not pointed out what's frivolous in the case before him before making those unlawful statements.

August 5, 2009

Sensei Rick Wilson is a fifth degree black belt in Tae Kwon Do karate at 4444 Forest Park Avenue and I am a security officer at the building. Sensei Wilson has a PHD in science and works in the Genome Center. Sometimes he invites me to a black belt test, and I talk with his students. Every Wednesday and Thursday morning Sensei teaches his students. Most of the mornings, I talk with him about the interesting events I wrote about in my book. Today, I spoke to Wilson about my experiences in practicing judo, and told him I achieved a ranking in judo under Sensei Bill Laud, who died several years ago. I told Wilson I'll put a section in my book on judo and Sensei Bill Laud in my book called the "The Making of a Black Belt Karate Champion." I guess I can start with the time I won the first place trophy at a judo tournament held at Forest Park Community College, and most of my wins came from choke holds, but my favorite technique was the hip throw. Another martial artist by the name of Greg, and I spent a lot of time discussing the martial arts. He was a Tae Kwon Do specialist. I tried to tell him not to telegraph his Filipino leg kicks because he took his eyes off his opponents. I showed Greg my pictures of the trophies I won in competition and got a chance to meet his wife who was an accountant.

August 6, 2009

I am getting ready for the August 25, 2009 small claims case, and I feel with the grace of God I'll be able to win. In my attempts to win the case, I found the old money order, because one of the opposing attorneys affirmative defenses would be, I do not have the original receipt, to match with the money order, which was whited out by the person, who took my money order and cashed it.

August 12, 2009

I took Candis's place and enjoyed talking to the employees starting to work at 5:30 a.m. I called Ethel and wished her well. I did not realize I took her water pills by mistake until I checked and took it back to her. I helped Latasha on making a decision on whether to attend cosmetology school. I gave her suggestions because she has a tourist business giving her income to pay for cosmetology school. I got into a debate with Jeff about President Obama's birthplace, and I said you cannot always go on news from the Enquirer. He did not tell me how he could prove President Obama was not born in the United States.

August 17, 2009

I called a martial arts publishing company and the officials said to send my book proposal and cover letter to them. When I got home, I wrote a query letter putting a rough together on what I wanted to say. The book includes a section on the many people who influenced my attitude as a martial artist. This book is unique because most of the martial artists I know do not publish their accomplishments in karate, judo, and other exciting events, when they win trophies in tournament competition.

I have not seen any books written by local martial artists in the St. Louis, Missouri area. That's something I wanted to do, and one day I'll write a book about the Midwest Martial Arts Association, I competed in.

August 21, 2009

I received the decision from the Eighth Circuit Appellate Court concerning the en banc order and the complaint against the Washington University Board of Trustees. The justices in the appellate court said eight justices in the lower court did not give me notice; they were making me do eight unconstitutional measures; so I could not comment on why they were unjust, before they made their decision to take this unlawful action against me. The appellate justices said the eight justices must show where in my pleadings, frivolous litigation was being written in my petitions, and they did not do this. The justice violated rule 85, and now I can file my cases without doing the mandated unconstitutional en banc order. The eight federal justices were appointed by the presidents of the United States. The judge said I could file a cause of action against Washington University located in St. Louis, MO.

August 21, 2009

I appeared in court with Judge Sweeny presiding and my attorney and attorney Buckingham were in attendance. I spoke to attorney Jarman and she told me Judge Sweeny wanted her to combine the first amended petition with the first petition so everything would be in one place and attorney Jarman said she would rewrite it.

August 23, 2009

I spoke to Cullen Cook and he said he was ready to get into singing. Taking an early retirement made him go into music. This en banc order made a great impact on my thoughts. I told a few people about the good news like Reggie, who's trying to get into law school, and a former classmate of mine, and Carla who wished me good luck and criticized me about not writing out a contract with Reverend Stevens because of the legal work I assisted him with. I told my mother about the victory, and she said I should get a lawyer, but I told her I would do the work myself. Donny and Kevin worked for Allied Barton, and I informed them about the appellate court decision. My good friends Charley, and Robert congratulated me on winning my appeal. Sherry Waller played an important role by informing me the eight federal judges signed the en banc order did not give me notice, before issuing their order to deny me the right to file cases in their federal court. I informed Eric Morris and he told his father Dan Morris about it too.

I spoke with my daughter Benica Pointer on August 28, 2009, and we talked about the Eighth Circuit Appellate Court decision, and how hard it was trying to write a consolidated brief for the first time. I pointed out several things concerning the importance of getting due-process when an en banc order is imposed without notice, and now I do not have to comply with the unconstitutional en banc order. I told my daughter how my letters to the board of trustees were kept from being sent to the board members to get them to investigate why I could not be admitted into the law school.

September 4-09

I sent in my summons and petition to the sheriff of Fairfax, Virginia because the writ might not go through. They gave me so many days to have the Naval Federal Credit Union served.

September 07, 2009

I received a response from the Eighth Circuit District Court. They gave me the rights to file my complaint against Washington University Board of Trustees. They are going to give me sixty days to respond to why I should not be given a prejudgment injunction against me. I spoke with Sherry and she said the lower federal court judges are acting as advocates for the defendants in the cases against me. The judges are singling me out, because I filed so many law suits, when other lawyers and prose litigants are doing the same thing, but this is disparate treatment against me because those same lawyers and Pro-Se are not subjugated to an en banc order.

October 31, 2009

I took my summons and petition to Division 29. After several times of turning in my summons and petition to judge Hogan I did the following things:

I studied a paternity petition done by child support officials who showed the names of the parties and their social security numbers on them and not their addresses. I looked at petitions filed by the court and it showed the same examples. I spoke to a lawyer and he said I could put their social security number on the party's names also. This time when I wrote out my petitions the lawyers did feel I could submit it without any problems. The clerk took my summons and petition to the judge and she came back and said my case was dismissed. I told the clerk I received a new case number and re filed the case. After that, the clerk came back and told me Judge Hogan told her to tell me to file my petition and summons in the clerk's office on the third floor. The problem is so many headings on petitions were submitted in this case it was difficult determining which one was the correct one. Mr. Hodgsons told me Venita's name was supposed to be on the petition, but the judge would not accept my petition because of it. The address of the Missouri Director of Family Services should be on the petition. I called the clerk in Division 29 and he said I would be hearing from the court.

I filed a request for damages in the case against Bertha for up to $ 150,000 dollars, because she lied at the hearing which took place over the phone, because she said I never sent her any support, but $ 11,000 dollars and higher was sent to her and the other people at the hearing had packets except me. I drew up a motion to add another party because child support had a hearing and should be considered a party to the litigation. I did not want to just have Bertha served and not them also. I filed an amended alias summons because I placed the child support address next to the Cole County Sheriff's Department next to it. This time the physical address and the mailing address were placed on the amended alias summons and three copies were sent to the court, and stamped with the appropriate date. On the alias summons, it stated the address at the Lewis and Clark Library would be used, because I could not get Bertha served at her address. I filed a motion to not have my case put on the November 5,2008 dismissal docket because the sheriff could not have her served at her house and St. Louis County officials would not cooperate with me when I tried to set up a time to have her subpoenaed to get her business address. I paid $ 30 dollars to have the Cole County Sheriff's Department serve Bertha.

Pointer v Parents for Fair Share

I applied for assistance in a program called Parents for Fair Share. Instead of them helping me get a job, they said I was too qualified to be helped by them, which I felt was discrimination, and should have been helped just like the other men. The only requirements were that you had to be 18 and a citizen of Missouri. This was disparate treatment against me because the other men were helped and not me. The case was sent to the 8th Circuit Appellate Court and the United States Supreme Court.

Pointer Teaching for Beacon Management

This case involved me going to a charter school, and they accepted my resume, and later called me to teach the fifth grade. The charter school was located on 4300 Good fellow in a red brick building. On the street heavy traffic ran up and down it and military vehicles. After reading my resume, Miss. Duckworth asked me if I wanted the job. The classroom did not look too good and many of the students did not have books. As I taught the students, I saw it was difficult teaching them, and they threw paper on the floor, or at each other. Trying to lecture to them posed several problems, because they wanted to do other things, instead of what I had to say.

To better teach my class, I arrived at school early in the morning, and placed the work on the board, so they could do it. While they worked, I made visits to each student, and saw what they were doing. At night I graded their papers and made lesson plans. To get to know my students consisting of African Americans, and one Asian girl student called Chinese, I sometimes spoke with them as a group. The students enjoyed art, and since I took 18 hours of art, I instructed them in this subject matter. For art, music, and computers, they went to separate classes. I received no evaluations from the administration, but I put half of the unruly students who did not want to learn in the hallway, and told the principal why, but they did not fire me. I told them I came here to teach and they were not going to run me away like they did the other teachers. I got to know my students because, I played team sports with them, and their other teachers did not. I passed all of my students, and was able to buy me a house, as a result of working at Thurgood Marshall Charter School.

Pointer v. Missouri Corrections

I graduated from the University of Missouri, St. Louis with a Bachelor of Science degree in Criminal Justice. After doing classwork from 1999 to 2001, and two summers; I completed the program, and applied for a job at the Missouri Corrections Department, and took their test, and passed it. I received a letter from them not explaining why I could not work for them when the job required only a high school diploma. My name was taken off the list without me knowing about it. Judge Limbaugh said I had felony and misdemeanor charges pending against me, and that's why he dismissed my case. Calling the St. Louis County Police, they informed me a mistake was made, and I sent this information to judge Limbaugh asking him to change the decision, but he refused to do it. The 8th Circuit Appellate Court ruled in my favor on my race discrimination claims, and dismissed the age discrimination claim. The case was remanded back to Judge Limbaugh's court where he dismissed it again. The same appellate panel of judges except one of the original said I was allowed to pursue an age discrimination claim. I attempted to get it to the United States Supreme Court, but it was too late when I submitted it. In my opinion, the appellate court had already ruled out the age discrimination claim when it was first heard by them, but the trial court on remand back to them dismissed it, saying I attempted an age discrimination claim, when I wrote out the EEOC form. In the form I pointed out that no non-discriminatory reason was given for not hiring me is an inference of discrimination.

CHAPTER 20

MY YEAR OF STUDY AT CONCORD ONLINE LAW SCHOOL 2010 TO 2011

I decided to attend law school the best way that I could, but the first step was back in 1999. I was rejected by 30 law schools and decided not to give up. Working two jobs, I served as a sales associate at Office Max for four hours a night to earn more money, and during the day I got employment with the Special School District to help pay application fees which cost $100 dollars at some law schools. Despite the setbacks, I enrolled at the University of Missouri, St. Louis, in their Bachelor of Science degree program, and took criminal justice courses, and graduated in June of 2002, and made the Dean's List. On May 26, 2010, I received a call from Dona Catalano, and she said I was accepted into the Concord Law School, and indicated it took three days for her to get in touch with me. I worked from 11 p.m. to 7.a.m in the morning, and went home to get some rest. At about 8:30 a.m., she called and said, "Are you sleeping Charles?"

I said, "Yes,"

"Well, I called you back," and she said, "Charles you have been accepted into the law school."

Immediately, I woke up and said," We can talk about it."

After years of trying to get into law school, I felt compelled to talk with her. I visited Forest Park Community College, and went to the administrative building at about 3:30 p.m. in the evening. I reviewed my e-mails, and saw what was needed to complete my application. The administrative lady faxed the financial aid form to the university. It did not say if they received the information or not. I went to the financial aid office and the same lady entered and gave me some trouble and denied me the opportunity to fax my financial aid package to Concord Law School. I asked the receptionist could I have them fax those documents to Concord Law School, and the lady told her no. That supervisor was angry because I went to her boss. The college could not deny me services if they are receiving federal funds, and the supervisor told me to come and see her, if I had any more problems with that worker. I enrolled in the Concord Law School which is on line and located in California. It was difficult trying to register for the law school because I did not have a computer, and traveled to various St. Louis area colleges to complete the application process. To pay for my courses, I received financial aid and was accepted after I passed a true and false exam on contracts, and I turned in an essay on why I wanted to attend law school. The courses I took were contracts, torts, and criminal law, and my instructor's name was Mr. Dodge, and he really taught us a lot of law in that year of study. Our lecture class was once a week and he gave us case law assignments, which we discussed in class. Professor Dodge posed several questions to us, and we supplied the answers, and if they were correct he listed them, and explained the pros and cons to them. To start the class, we signed in, and he played opera music before his lectures started, and checked to see if we were hearing him speak. At the start of class, Professor Dodge wrote long paragraphs of law which he wanted us to know about to help us with our exams. Outside of this class activity, we had lectures on the same topics by two other professors, and we took notes on the materials. We took weekly programed exams every week, and my modules as they were called consisted of at least 30 in each of the areas of law we studied. I enjoyed studying the law and interacting with my classmates; you could not see the students but there was a web site with all of your classmates' pictures on it, and what they majored in as an undergraduate student. If you had problems, you always called your advisor for help. They taught us how to examine the facts of the case and set law to it, and methods of answering multiple choice questions too. I passed the torts, criminal law, and contracts part of the exam, even though I had two and one half hours to do the essay part and the other students three and a half hours. The tech person took thirty minutes to log me in for my exam, and I complained, and another administrative officer logged me. My grades would have been higher if I would have been given more time to complete the exam. I did not get a chance to take the first state exam in California, and took out a loan for this purpose which I am making payments on now. By going to this law school the training helped me in future cases when I went to court.

CHAPTER 21

MORE LITIGATION AS PRO-SE ATTORNEY
9-25-010

I paid the light bill which was $75 dollars, gas bill $200 dollars, $50 dollars for internet service, $25 dollars sewer bill, and $50 dollars for the telephone bill. I have begun writing out my writ of certiorari for the United States Supreme Court. At first I had problems doing it, but I was able to buckle down and actually use the software. I was going to let Carla's daughter do it first but something like this is a specialty which I wanted to do myself. Now I am happy I undertook the responsibility to do the work to learn from the experience.

May 20, 2010

My daughter Kalah visited the tiny island country called Haiti with her classmates, and they all attended Joplin Christian College. She sent me some pictures of the people she met in that country. One picture showed where a lady was washing her clothes with her hands, a picture of two curious looking kids, and some of her friends who went to Haiti with her.

May 20, 2010

Today just was not my day but I started off by feeding my dog Black. I typed the appendix only to discover that you must put the original copies of the appendix in the brief. I tore up what I wrote on the appendix. To have Venita served, I would have to pay $ 48 dollars and the Missouri Division of Family Services $ 30 dollars. I went to Forest Park Community College to retrieve information left on my e-mail by Dona Catalano, who is my admissions advisor at Concord Law School. I drove to the University of Missouri, St. Louis and ran into a curve and busted a hole in my tire. A University of Missouri policeman came by and asked if he could help me. I said," That's ok I have to put on a donut tire."

Later a lady who worked in the library stopped and asked if I could call an emergency number for help.

I said, "I got it under control and all I have to do is put the donut on the axle."

After getting the tire on, I decided to complete my task of getting the information from my e-mail pertaining to the software. Before going to the library, I climbed a steep hill about half the length of a football field. Being very tire, I managed to get up the hill and went to the library. I found the software requirements on my e-mail and realized I did not have any paper to write on, so I asked a librarian to get some scratch paper, so I could copy the information down. Concord Law School is an elite online law school requiring its candidates to have a Bachelor of Science degree to be admitted. After I wrote down the information, I looked for United States Supreme Court cases. On the way home, I made a left turn and went into a sub-division to avoid being stopped by the police to see if I had car insurance or was driving while intoxicated. With all the problems I faced this morning, I did not want to be bothered with paying court costs for any of those reasons if stopped by the police; I made my way to highway 70 through the subdivision and entered St. Louis, MO.

6-3-010

Today I spoke with Dona Catalano and told her I would go to the Forest Park Community College to e-mail an administrator at Concord to send me a college expense form. Most of the week I've been eating rice and vegetables. I had my problems with the financial aid officials who did not want to help me because I was not a student enrolled in their college. I went to the financial aid officer and she told me if I had financial aid problems she would tell her workers to help me. This was a federal program and her people could not avoid helping me. Later that day I went out to the Marco Computer Company and bought my lap top and printer. To get financial assistance, I went to Arrow Finance and got the money. I thought I knew where the company was located but I rode several miles passed it and traveled to the library to get the correct address. Once I got the right address, I reached the company and filled out the papers even though I needed my glasses.

June 6, 2010

I did some work on my United States Supreme Court brief due on July 1,2010. At first, I wrote out the questions to be presented. Later, I found out through research that an introduction was needed, so I wrote one to each question to be presented. I felt much better because I could see a clear picture of what I was attempting to do.

June 12, 2010

I called the telephone service so they could come out and fix the wires. My first lecture at Concord Law School took place at 12 o'clock central standard time. Earlier I went to the food pantry on Dr. Martin Luther King Avenue and they referred me to Antioch Church on West Market not too far from Homer G. Philips Hospital. At first I went down Martin Luther King Drive going too far East with hardly any gas in my car. I drove back home to hear the lecture, but it was an awful experience because I could not get a dial tone from my phone. I went to the alley and saw where the trash truck driver knocked the telephone pole down. Going to Mrs. Watt's house, I asked her if I could call the internet people from her house. I could not get internet service because the trash truck lifted our trash dumpster too high and tore down some telephone wires. Monday I'll call Archway Communications to come out and fix the wires for me. They might cut off the gas; hopefully I'll get out of this dilemma and get back on my feet. The road to becoming a lawyer is a rough one but I'll never give up my dream. The God I worship will never forsake me. I let Black eat a loaf of bread Mrs. Watt gave me. It was helpful because I did not have any food to eat.

6-26-010

I embarked on a journey of completing law school. I have to get the multiple choice questions studied and go back to the fundamental class on that subject matter. It was difficult trying to get everything done. The Concord people said they attempted to contact me for three days trying to get me enrolled into their law school after I was accepted. I received financial aid and paid $ 700 dollars for my books and that was accomplished from getting my money back when a company cashed my money order using fraud and a case my personal injury attorney settled for me.

July 17, 2010

I was fortunate enough to get an extension to file out of time to file my writ of certiorari and I did not have the money to have my writ copied. I wrote the court and explained my problem and how I was treated by trial court when they did not have Washington University served and they were not made a party to the case as a result of this. I said the lower court did not tell me when it was going to issue an injunction against me without notice. I received a letter from the court clerks indicating they would extend the time to August 30, 2010. I explained in my letter that I met a lot of expenses getting accepted into Concord Law School and could not pay the money to have my writ copied and printed. Sherry said I should frame any correspondence pertaining to Justice Alito of the United States Supreme Court because he looked at my issues which took place in the lower court and were presented to their higher court.

I presented to the lower state court my motion for a default judgment against Venita Washington and The Missouri Division of Family Services. Venita was served on June 2, 2010 and The Missouri Division of Family Services on May 26 and neither of them responded.

July 24, 2010

Now I am engaged in the pursuit of completing my training as an attorney with Concord Law School. I enjoy the lectures and feedback received from Professor Dodge. He gives lectures on the different topics and feedback from the questions we study on the subject matter. I've placed many of the torts on flashcards and will have them memorized by June 2011. The lectures are reinforced by lectures from other professors.

October 15, 2010

I attempted to write out my writ again and this time I started with Statement of The Case and will complete Why the Writ Should Be Granted. I decided to have this section on a different page since all I have to do is number them from one to the conclusion of the writ. I will go back to the beginning and do those on a different web site.

Reverend Stevens came over on the 14th of October and we made plans to meet on the 15th but the trash truck ran into the telephone wires knocking them down leaving me without a telephone to use.

November 5, 2010

I went to Office Depot on November 5, 2010 and requested that Carl Laws copy my writ of certiorari to the United States Supreme Court and he refused to copy it stating I got the copies from another service. He did not treat the other people like me who came and had their work printed but not mine. Carl tried to tell me what was wrong with my writ which is the responsibility of the clerks at the court and not him. Carl said something about a policy they had about copying material, but failed to show it to me when I requested it. I asked Madeleine, who was the manager about this policy, but she did not tell me what the policy was, but other people got their work copied, without Carl or her questioning them about the subject matter of their projects. Plaintiff is saying his First and Fourteenth Amendments were violated by Carl and Madeleine when they did not copy my writ. I feel disparate treatment took place because I was the only one who was treated like this. The job discrimination agencies I tried to get help from ruled against me. I was too busy trying to get my writ to the United States Supreme Court submitted and was too busy to file this case to federal court for discrimination. Getting my writ to the high court took a lot of my time from getting that Office Depot complaint filed in federal court.

November 13, 2010

I sent my brief to the United States Supreme Court. The writ was the same size on its fonts but when it was reduced it changed to a lower one. I hope my writ will not be dropped as a result of it. In the book it stated that filing in forma pauperis they wanted the writ to come as close to specification as possible. I wrote a letter explaining why the font was not the same size after they made it 6'9" size. I requested that this was an important document because the issues I presented constituted a violation of my 14th, 4th, and First Amendment rights.

June 5, 2011

Now, as I write in this point of my life, I find myself in a dilemma. Concord Law School kept me from logging into their law school for about two weeks. The law school said it was Charter Communications' fault and Charter said it was the law school's fault. Charter said I was getting internet service and that was their only obligation to me. Scot who worked in tech support said it was Charter Communications who was not clearing its proxy servers. E-machines did a test and determined it was the law school that was not letting me log into the school. It took thirty minutes to log into the essay part of the final after dealing with Scot who worked in tech support at Concord. I called the administration and said Scot's behavior showed he did not like black people. An administrator logged me into the web site to start my part of the exam. I did not get equal time on each part of the essay components on torts, criminal law, and contracts. I made a c+, c- and d+ on my essays despite I did not get enough time to write on the essay section showing how I got my answer leading to a conclusion. My grades on the essay section would have been higher if I would have been given equal time on the essay part of the exam. Regardless of the situation, I tried to overcome the frustrations of arguing with Scot who took very little time to help me. After the essay exam, I did the multiple choice part on it. I could not finish the two hundred question exam by 5:30 p.m. because I was supposed to be at work by 5:30 p.m., even after the college officials gave me until 6 p.m. to finish the exam. The next day I received an e-mail stating for me to turn in the multiple choice questions for grading. A breach of contract took place when they said I turned in the multiple choice questions too late. To be fair, I feel my multiple choice questions should have been graded to see if I passed the final. They did not tell me until June 1, 2011 I would not be certified to take the first year law exam. By doing this, the time to get a full refund from the $ 564 dollars I paid to take the test expired. I requested the Missouri Attorney General's Office to check into what took place, and they said they could not represent me as an attorney, but would investigate the problem, and offer a solution. I contacted a lawyer and left a message for him to call me. I spoke to the attorney and he listened to me and said for me to come in and see him. I told him I would come downtown to show him how I broke down the case using the IRAG method I learned at the law school.

September 2011

I went to McDonalds Hamburgers and as usual I promoted my book called "The Making of a Black Belt Karate Champion", and the fellows really loved the way I explained what the book was about. I pointed out some of the humorous things that made people cry in tears of laughter. I spoke about Ken's method of telling me the fight would be over in two seconds when it appeared I would have to fight coach in one of the tournaments, we went to. The referees placed us in two different weigh classes and sensei took first place, and I won the second place trophy. I discussed with them when I told Ken I fought Larry Tankston, before I knew he was a four time world champion, and Ken said if I knew he was a four time world champion; I would not have come out to fight him. My publisher representative said whoever reads my book will enjoy it. At first when I saw the message, I lost it, but after searching and finding the communications, I felt good about her positive comments. This was my first review from a representative associated with Xlibris, who published the book. In most of my conversations, I spoke to people about the book to promote it, and many of them said they would buy it. On Monday, I was part of a group of security officers who patrolled the streets going east of Skinker Avenue because of the robberies which took place in the Washington University area, and many students and residents living there listened to me talk about my book, and I told them I graduated from Washington University School of Journalism in 1985.

10-14-011

Now I am in the middle of sending $ 175 dollars to the city of St. Louis after my attorney got the court case waived, and no points were issued against my driver's license. I hated paying the fine because the money could be used to pay for the corrections in my book. I spoke to Jesse Klinger, and she said the first corrections were free to be placed in the book, but the next ones I would have to pay for them. Many people I spoke to about the book were elated when I discussed different aspects of it. If I ever have to talk with people about my book, I'll high light the humorous sections first, where Ken jokes about his adventures, and his karate experiences. We laughed so hard and loud at McDonalds Hamburgers, one of the managers threatened to put us out. I paid the money to have everything corrected and I read books on Ernest Hemingway like "For Whom the Bell Tolls" and books on marketing.

10-20-011

I worked at Washington University and it paid off. Many robberies took place on the streets bordering Skinker. It was difficult at first walking down the street in leather shoes. My goal was to make some money and pay for editing my book. This assignment was left up to the authors who wrote their books which were fiction or nonfiction. I read a final galley and sent in twenty one errors. I did not realize they corrected the forty errors I sent to them. The $225 dollars came into question after I realized they put the corrections in the book before I paid the money. Everything was done to my satisfaction.

November 3, 2011

I spoke to Miss. Jesse Klinger at Xlibris Publishing and she said my book would be in print very soon. This was exciting news to hear after months of writing and going over the manuscript. Earlier I stopped by a book store owner and he said I could have a book signing at his store, which was located on Manchester. The book store was dark on the inside and he had red lights on the windows. He said Xlibris published many black writers and people did not care who published the book. He said in a book signing the author and bookstore owner shared the money made from the event. I stopped at the Left Bank Bookstore, and he said to bring the book to them so they could review it, and later have a book signing. I think I have a winner in that I will market the book in many venues. I chose to not tell anyone about what Miss. Klinger told me. Sometimes it's best not to do this. I am thinking about arguing this case against Office Depot myself, or see if I can get a lawyer to do it. I do not get alone with lawyers all the time. I broke down the case using the IRAG method. It's a matter of disparate treatment, because Carl Lewis had no right to not copy my writ, but copied other customer's projects, and did not question them about them. No company policies were given to justify why my writ could not be copied.

November 15, 2011

Now, I am getting chiropractor treatments from Dr. Humphrey. On November the 10, 2011 I was hit in the rear end of my car by a motorist. My neck was injured in the process. I went to a nearby telephone, and called the police, and he made a report, but the other driver did not have any insurance card, only his motorist card. Bob and I tried to buy parts for his car. The problem is he bought a starter on the recommendations of friends and he only needed an ignition switch. I went to Grace hill and Dr. Jacquelyn examined me, and I told her my neck was stiff, and I could turn it slowly. She gave me some pain killers, and one pill for my neck, and applied physical therapy to relieve the pain.

I received a call from child support saying since I did not call the hearing officer on the 14th, indicating I could not make the hearing; it would be dismissed. On the 13th, I called customer service, and told them I could not make the hearing because I had to work, and would they ask the hearing officer to reschedule. They documented they contacted the enforcement team and told them about it.

November 19, 2011

Now I am trying to finish my book, "The Making of a Black Belt Karate Champion", and I always have to correct the manuscript. I sent a final galley to the publishers and I enjoyed speaking with Miss. Jesse Klinger, who gave nothing but good compliments about the way they were working on my manuscript. I think I might start taking more photographs and writing poetry to them, and giving an interpretation about them. I am writing a novel called "A Time to Remember" about life in the Southern part of the United States in a time period of 1950 leading into the civil rights period of the 1960's of an interracial love affair. I read several books on writing like Jack London's "Call of the Wild" and books by Ernest Hemmingway. I am getting in the habit of eating healthier foods. In my early sixties, I decided to be more productive and become a writer and get into a law school. Some of the people I knew came and asked me legal questions, and I tried to help them, but requested they consult with a lawyer after talking with me. The cleaning crew and I enjoyed debating about many topics, and especially the subjects of law, and politics, and many of them were very smart when talking about something they knew about.

November 30, 2011

Last night I was in a bad mood because I thought I lost the rewritten copy of my book Called "A Time to Remember" because I did not find the rewritten part of the first part which was one hundred and fifty pages. I tore the house upside down looking for it. I begin to get suspicious of the people who came around my desk at 4444 Forest Park where I worked as a security officer. Some people liked to call us guards, but the title they put on our licenses is security officer. Many security officers have degrees and some of them don't, and come from academic backgrounds in law enforcement. Sometimes I have to educate people on how important security is, and I have a Bachelor of Science degree in Criminal Justice from Missouri University, St. Louis, MO, Class of 2001. Their criminal justice program is ranked number one in the United States. In my courses, I wrote papers on DNA and The Death Penalty, Girl Gangs in Missouri, and School Security. It was amazing to see how people felt about freeing people placed in jail that did not deserved to be there. This was the first time I enjoyed studying statistics, which showed how people in different racial, economic incomes, and educational categories were in favor, or not in favor of the use of DNA in letting people be innocent, or in the other case guilty of different crimes, whatever the case may be.

November 29, 2011

I went over to Olin Hall and spoke with Reggie who was twenty five years old and he wanted to get his criminal justice degree, but because his work shift changed regularly; he attended school online, and Reggie said he wanted to be finished by the time he was thirty years old.

I said, "Reggie, stop thinking about the age requirement because you lose interest if you put a time limit on your ability to succeed, or not succeed."

I told him about the people, who influenced me in my early process of getting a good education like, Dr. Howard Miller, who I met at O'Fallon Technical High School, after getting out of Boonville School of Reformatory, and earned his PHD, and won a Danforth Fellowship. I told him Howard was African American, and came from a large family, and grew up in the low income parts of the black community, but this did not stop his dream of becoming something important in life, and he taught college for thirteen years. One of those years I went to Defiance, Ohio to visit him and his family. Years later I sat in on a class of his when he taught sociology classes at Southern Illinois University at Edwardsville, Illinois. I explained to Reggie about my earlier life of living in Meachum Park which was a low income part of Kirkwood, Missouri, and how I was introduced to Truman Chiles, a Caucasian, who enrolled me into college, and paid for my first courses, and Mr. Jones an African American, who got me a job at Bemis Bags located in Fenton, Missouri. To make my story more interesting, I told Reggie about meeting an African American executive by the name of Peter, who happened to be walking through the plant in a nice suit, and he and I spoke to each other, and Peter told me he was in management training. I further told Reggie, Peter informed me he graduated from college, and I could do the same thing if I wanted to;that I got tire of being dirty all day getting ink on my clothes, and left that company, and enrolled in college as a fulltime student, at Forest Park Community College, and earned six degrees, and a specialized certificate in journalism. To inspire other students traveling in my direction, I told them what it was like achieving success trying to graduate from all the colleges I attended.

December 5, 2011

Today I got a check for $ 2,013 dollars because a motorist ran into the back of my car. My neck and back were injured, and the bumper and gas cap were damaged.

The driver got out of his car and said, "I know the game. You are feeling your neck like it is hurt!"

He did not realize my neck got injured as a result of the accident. When his vehicle hit my back fender my neck went back and forth several times, and Bob's skull cap fell off his head. At first, I called a policeman to come and make a report and later I went to the chiropractor, Dr. Humphrey. He immediately applied treatments to my back and neck. At Grace hill, Dr. Hill examined my neck, and back, and gave me some pain pills. I could not turn my head too quickly. Hopefully, I can use the money to help with the marketing phrase of my book which cost $ 500 dollars. I sent my papers to Thomas Jefferson Law School which is online, and ABA accredited, and took Sharon to the hospital to get a knee replacement operation.

December 11, 011

Today I got off to a wonderful start at 2:30 a.m.in the morning, I listened to music by a group called Sole Children made up of two girls and two boys. They singed beautiful music, and I saw Smokey Robinson singing with two gospel groups paying tribute to Sam Cooke, and he singed the song "You Send Me" first recorded and written by Cooke.

Luther Vandross singed a melody of songs written by Smokey when he was placed into the Rock in Roll Hall Of Fame. I called Sharon and Ethel and we talked about many topics. I asked Sharon if a company can change the answers in a computer I marked, when I applied for a job at Home Depot, and she said yes. To keep my mind active, I read a book on Ray Charles, and his relationship with a lady, who lived in Kirkwood, Missouri, when I stayed in that town. Their relationship lasted for thirty years, and at that time; I started writing my novel "A Time to Remember."

December 15, 2011

I took my test to renew my security license, to continue to work as a security officer, and about one hundred other officers appeared at the test site to do the same thing. If you came in passed 8:15 p.m., they told you to go back home. I remember one person coming in late, and he could not take the test, and rescheduled to take it again. The security officer taught us many things about being safe when working at your post. Wearing blue jeans were not allowed, or hats. If an officer missed more than eight questions, the person administering the test said you could not get your license renewed.

In the lecture, the officer said you must notify the local police if a problem took place, you could not handle yourself. Other areas of concern were: You had to put your weapon in a trunk when leaving your job. You must have probable cause to arrest someone, and many other important things. I passed the test with no problems, but I took notes also.

December 15, 2011

I saw this fellow coming up to the fence and he said," I like this dog. I can take him home today." My dog Black did not take his behavior too lightly, when he placed his finger on the fence, and he snapped at it, because Black does not get too friendly with people he does not know. This wild behavior is part of his breed because he is a pit bull, and Black got angry when he could not attack the fellow, teasing him. Trying to use store bought chains became impossible because Black broke them. Still attempting to complete my book, I sent last minute corrections to officials at Xlibris Book Publishers. Eating breakfast at McDonalds, I spoke with Bernard about giving the officials at Xlibris my credit card information, and he said I have to be careful because money can be taken out of your account without you knowing it. A humorous incident took place at McDonalds Hamburgers, when a fellow came to the restaurant, and tried to sell some belts, and Bernard said he could not buy anything without a price tag on it.

The other brother who sat down with us said, "I do not see any sales tags on the belts, or any brand names on them either." What the fellow said was so funny the customers laughed their hearts out about this fellow trying to sell the belts.

December 16, 2011

On this particular day at McDonalds Hamburgers, me and the fellows talked about black actors playing in motion pictures as big stars, instead of the slave, cook, or porter roles, and they loved to see black people playing in roles that made them heroes. I told them my book, "The Making of a Black Belt Karate Champion," was still being worked on, and they kept harassing me about when it would be completed. I bought some new pipes for my sink because the original ones were corroded, and I stopped water from coming out of the pipes, when the old ones were replaced. I saw it was difficult trying to get lawyers to handle my discrimination cases. Many of the lawyers tried to be judge and jury before taking the case, and sometimes you have to get lawyers from another state to represent you, instead of the local ones. A driver drove his motor vehicle into the back of my car, and I am getting paid compensation after the chiropractor treats my back and neck.

December 19-2011

I saw the clips of my first press release for my book. The people who wrote it took certain parts of my book and incorporated it into the press release which impressed me. They showed me 148 newspapers the press release was shown in. The writers of the press releases captured the spirit in which I wrote the book, and it made me very happy when I saw it.

December 19, 2011

I did a number of things to make my life comfortable. I am taking more vitamin c in the form of grapefruit and oranges. I researched and it indicated vitamin c lowers high blood pressure. On the 16th of December, I scrambled through the hallway for about fifteen minutes. Most of the time I walked a half an hour in the hallways, and it kept my waist lean and trim. I spoke to Rico Pago about my marketing plan, and he assured me my visa card number would be protected, and their company polices said I had to use my debit card. Rico said this press release would be sent to two hundred newspapers in the United States. This was a good year for me, because I received $1500 dollars from an automobile accident, when someone hit my car. A car ran into the back of mine, and I am getting paid for damages, after the chiropractor treats my back and neck. I kept the two thousand dollars instead of fixing dents in my car, I can live with. I'll get a vacation buyout at the end of the year. I am making headway with my novel called "A Time to Remember" and doing a rewrite of the first version, and keeping a daily journal helps me with my writing. It's like doing an exercise but the only thing you are doing is writing, which helps to improve the manner, in which you express yourself, in written communication. On December 17, 2011, I stopped by Mike Novels and watched his students practice. I enjoy getting up early in the morning to do my writing. A representative from Xlibris by the name of Rico Pigoe said, he would try to get my book to movie producers. I enjoyed reading a book on Canada Lee an African American who established success as a boxer, band leader, actor, and played in the motion picture "Cry the Beloved Country." The exciting thing about this is I owned the video, and watched it many times for relaxation, and I studied different aspects of the film, and attempted to learn how the film producers made it interesting. To fight Jim Crow laws associated with prejudice, Canada Lee worked with civic groups to get positive roles for black actors instead of servants, or playing a slave, in many of the pictures; they made into motion pictures.

December 20, 2011

Today, I wrote a letter to the hearing section of child support, because I called the customer service department in Jefferson City, and told them I had to work 16 hours on October 14, 2011, and could not attend it. I called customer service on 10-13-011, and they called the enforcement team, and told them about it, but they failed to notify the hearing section. This letter went out certified to the Jefferson City hearing section requesting a hearing date and I would take legal action, and use breach of contract, and due-process as a cause of action. The funniest thing happened at work when Obdeed a fellow who was from Africa wanted to know more about my book called, "The Making of a Black Belt Karate Champion." Bernice said she would buy the book if I brought a copy of it to my job site, which I did not want to do, because I could get fired for trying to sell books.

December 22, 2011

I completed 48 corrections on my manuscript, and sent them to Xlibris so they could be incorporated into the book. I have written many corrections into the final manuscript. The press release was ready and I sent it in. Today, I will write on my novel "A Time to Remember" and hope to get it published. I might change the title of that book. I've decided to have a career in law and writing. I spoke to Andy, who is in the Physical Therapy program, about taking pictures; so I can write a travel piece, when he visits different parts of the United States.

January 4, 2012

I got up early in the morning and thought it was 9:00 p.m. in the evening, but it was in the morning. I called Ethel and she told me it was 9:a.m. in the morning. I did my exercises from the Boom Boom Exercise Video Tapes, but stopped when he kept going too fast on the jump rope section of the tape. I visited Mrs. Peppers, who works at the clinic I go to, and left a press release with her. She is a great supporter of mine who was impressed with me writing my book.

January 8, 2012

When I was a student in paralegal school and Concord Law School, I studied my lessons at the desk at 4444, even though I took care of my job responsibilities. During the Christmas holiday's drivers dropped off donuts and asked if we wanted one. Joe and Cheryl sometimes came to work together because she did not live too far from him. In some cases Joe and I discussed social problems with each other, and he is a great friend of mine. Little Willie John was an African American I read about.

January 13, 2012

I got off work and Bunny was in a humorous manner got on my case because she said," Charles with all of those degrees you got; you could have given your dog a better name then Black."

I said in a joking form of behavior, "his name is Black and I do not see anything wrong with his name."

I said, "Have you ever heard James Brown shout," Say it loud, I am black and I'm proud, or that black is beautiful?"

Denise, Robert, Steve, Van, and Bernice laughed as we joked about my dog's right to be called Black.

This final year of 2012 consisted of getting my book, "The Making of a Black Belt Karate Champion," published and going to karate class at Forest Park Community College. I kept a journal of how Sensei Williams instructed his class. I looked forward to attending the morning classes on Tuesdays and Thursdays from 8.a.m. to 9a.m. My dog Black got into problems, and he broke all of the dog leashes I put on him, and he kept digging holes in the ground, and crawling under a wire fence. I kept going next door to bring him back to my yard. For activities, I took Black on long walks, which helped to keep my blood sugar and pressure down. When Black broke his chains, I went looking for him in my car. But he always came back home if I could not find him. With his keen sense of smell, I came home late at night, and Black knew I was present and barked without seeing me.

After completing my year of law school at Concord on line law school, other on line schools tried to recruit me, but I wanted to attend a law school with students in a classroom setting. The online school experienced was great because the instructors taught me torts, criminal law, and contracts which I liked. Professor James Dodge taught with much love for his students because he put so much in his lectures, and his class sessions, and we sent in responses to his questions. During the spring of 2012, I spent much time promoting my book by going to Tri-light Tuesdays and passed out press releases to visitors who came to Jefferson Memorial located on Lindell Avenue at Forest Park in Saint in Louis, Missouri, to listen to local artists, and their music, performing it on stage. They were eager to hear good music by performers doing their renditions of soul music depending on what type of music they singed like pop, heavy metal, or country western, or rap. As many visitors sat and listened to the music, sitting in their lawn chairs on the green grass, I showed them my book and press releases, and explained what the book was about.

A fellow who worked for Washington University and drove a supply truck stopped, and said he bought the book, and skipped to the chapters which interested him, and he enjoyed reading it.

He said, "Charles I keep for getting to bring the book up here so you can sign it."

Sharon said she liked my writing style and the subject matter I injected into the book. Many people come to a weight lost and by-pass clinic at 4444 Forest Park where I worked at, and when I escorted them to where they should go, I talked with them about my book "<u>The Making of a Black Belt Karate Champion</u>", and discussed where they could buy it. This was a goal I tried to reach by explaining to them; they could overcome medical problems of trying to lose weight, and live a productive life by exercising and eating properly. I told them I was forty one when I trained and competed in karate tournaments against boys who were twenty years younger than me, which gave much encouragement to them to lose weight.

During the summer of 2012, a library administrator by the name of Carolyn, at the Julia Davis Library, invited me to attend their program called" Write On Writers." The person who sponsored the program was wonderful, and I appreciated her for inviting me to speak about the difficult journey I took to get my book published.

Seeing those people in the audience made me feel good they took the time out of their busy schedules to come and ask me questions on how I got my book published. They could have been doing something else with their lives instead of listening to what I had to say. One author in the group had about eight or nine books published. Some people wanted to know if I made much money on the book, and I chose not to talk about that because I do writing for the joy of it, and if the book sells, I'll be happy but my goal is to keep writing a good book first, not concentrating on monetary reward.

At 4444 Forest Park where I work as a security officer, I meet many people and enjoy my evenings talking with the janitorial crew about civic events and sports. I talked with a fellow from the Congo who spoke French and was a school teacher in his native country by the name of Desoluka, and I told him I would teach him English if he gave me French lessons. One of the janitorial staff by the name of Denise Ford had a good talent for cooking, and sometimes brought some home cooked food to help celebrate the holidays with her co-workers.

During Black Studies Month of February, Ethel put together a program to celebrate it by having members of the janitorial group give presentations on African Americans who made contributions to American culture. The Washu-Five organized by Ethel sang at the event, and the group consisted of Van, Denise, Wilma, Jackie, and Eugene who was going to college to become a coach of basketball. The janitorial crew contributed to the event by bringing food to eat.

When writing my book, I made business connections with people, and called the library, and proofread it for correct usage of proper English.

In the wee hours of the morning, while I wrote on my book at work, the Steve Harvey show aired, and he started his show by saying, "Steve Harvey has a radio show," several times before talking to the radio audience. As he said this, I could hardly keep my eyes open, and I said to myself maybe I could approach people and promote my book in the same manner. I stood up and kept saying 'I have a published book out called, "<u>The Making of a Black Belt Karate Champion</u> by Charles Pointer."

I approached different people with the same motivation Steve Harvey announced his show with, and this inspired me to keep on accomplishing my goals, especially when Steve emphasized keeping faith in God to make the impossible come true only if you believed in him.

Many janitorial crew members discussed child support issues, and I felt a man should support his kids, but I felt both parents should be in court when the matter is litigated in court. I did not have this opportunity when my ex-wife went to court. I was served to appear in court, however, I asked judge Huff, if I could get counsel and she gave me permission to get one, but Venita went to court anyway without giving me notice. I did not get a notice to appear in court on March 7th 1990 to take part in the divorce, and I felt this was wrong because Judge Grady did not know if I could afford to pay $ 500 dollars a month, which was awarded to Venita, but later changed to $ 200 a month for support, after I kept ligating the case in court. I told a worker you must pay child support even if you remarry. I said a parent must make a motion for modification if the child support is too large or not enough brought on by a change of circumstances. I still have an open case because my attorney said the judges kept passing my case to different court divisions, but I did not let this get me down, because I have not seen my kids in eight or nine years, but I still continued to pay child support, and they were taken to another state.

CHAPTER 22

THE REELECTION OF PRESIDENT BARACK OBAMA NOVEMBER 6, 2012.

On November 6, 2012, I witnessed the re-election of President Barack Obama 44th president of the United States and enjoyed witnessing the first time an African American was re-elected president of the United States of America in a highly competitive campaign by the challenger former governor of Massachusetts Mitt Romney. I went to the voting polls which were at Hickey Grade School. Outside the polling place canvassers gave you the Democratic slate of candidates running for the president of the United States, the United States senate seat from Missouri, St. Louis, Missouri local candidates, and states offices such as governor running for political office in the state of Missouri. I showed them my voter registration information and they gave me a ballot to vote on the candidates from the Democratic and Republican ticket. I voted for all the Democrats on the ballot of candidates. I voted for my friend Anthony Stevens, who ran for the Green Party for the Treasurer's Office for the city of St. Louis, Missouri. President Obama did not carry Missouri but he won the other states with the most electoral votes. The news casters showed Romney winning in the southern states but President Obama won the election winning the majority of the electoral votes. The election officials checked to see that people were being serviced to vote in a timely manner. I fell asleep before the election was over and woke up to see that President Obama was re-elected president of the United States. I enjoyed watching the debates between the two candidates and my candidate President Barack Obama won re-election to serve four more years.

CHAPTER 23

BEAUTIFUL MEMORIES OF MY KIDS

One part of my life I missed was not being around my four kids as they grew up, but I want to dedicate this section of my book to them, because I treasured the times we share together which were dear to me. Their names were Michelle, Kalah, Benica, and Charles Junior. I can start with Charles Junior born in 1976 when I was married to his mother. By the time I arrived at Homer G Philips Hospital his mother named him Charles Everett Pointer. When we lived on 4709 Davison, Charles began walking. Taking trips to Mississippi, we always took Charles with us. He gradually began talking and making sounds with words. Every evening before I bought a car, I caught the bus, and went to buy his milk because his mother did not breast feed him. When we moved to St. Louis County, we enrolled Charles into a nursery school. Sister Catherine spent much time teaching him his basic courses in reading, and writing, and eighteen years later, I took him to see her when he graduated from high school, and got a job. One evening, I drove near a Lincoln-Toyota car dealership, and stopped to look at some cars. Charles cried when I told him I could not immediately take the car home with me because business matters must take place first before I could be the owner of the car. At the age of four, he did not understand what high financing was about when it came to buying a car. (Smile)

At the close of the evening, I went and picked him up. I made sure he knew about African American history, because I was a history teacher and wanted him to know about the cultures of different races of people, which came to America, and made it into a strong nation called the United States of America. Being separated from his mother made it difficult to see him because, of his mother's negative attitude. I brought money out to him so he could go to field trips, because Charles played in the high school band at Riverview Gardens High School. I attended the middle school when he was in a contest to get first seat in the trumpet section in the band. I felt proud being there to see him compete. Having a noticeable walk, as he strolled down the hallways at school; he took broad steps leaning his body back and forth as he walked. Because of his style of walking, the senior class called him Cool Breeze, and he received an award from his graduating class for it. Part of my employment life involved teaching, and one evening Charles Junior was in the class, and his classmates asked him if I was his father, and he said yes.

Later Charles Junior said to me, "My friend told me you inspired him when he saw you were African American and a college graduate from good quality academic institutions."

Through the years, Charles Junior visited me, and witnessed me living in a cold house, when he brought me some money, which was a great help, because over half of my check was garnished for child support from two ex-wives, but he saw I remained in good spirits as I fought child support authorities in court, and got it lowered. Money came out of my check, but I never got a chance to visit him, or take him out with me to a movie or social outing. I criticized him for spending more time with my brother, and his sons, and after that I have not heard from him in about four years.

Benica came into the world in 1984 and her sister Kalah in 1985, and Venita was their mother. At that time before Benica's birth, Howard and his wife left, and Venita's water burst and I drove her to the hospital, and as I rushed down the highway Venita kicked, and screamed all the way to the operating room. It amazed me to see childbirth for the first time in my life. Benica was a bundle of joy, and I enjoyed being around her. I remember Benica trying to learn how to walk, and saw her take her first steps. Her pretty dark skin and white teeth glowed when you looked at her. Her sister Kalah came into the world in 1985, when I graduated from Washington University.

When we lived on Shaw Avenue, I worked from 11:p.m. in the morning at Stake and Shake to 7:a.m. in the morning, and before I left to go to work Venita, and I fed them while they sat in their high chairs, and I kissed them goodbye, and could not wait to see them, when I came home in the morning. I did not want to leave them, but I could not live with a woman who did not love me. Not being with my kids hurt and I thought about them, when we were apart from each other. I tried many times to see them, and retained the services of a lawyer to get visitation rights to see my children, but Venita did not comply with the court approved agreement to bring them to juvenile court so I could see them. I remember seeing them about eight years later at my mother's house, and I went and got a money order for one hundred dollars and gave it to their mother. About nine years later in 2001, I received a call from my daughters, and I went out to see them and immediately I bought clothes and food for them. I did not have to have a court order to make me take care of my children but despite my efforts to be a father and provide for my children, Venita went to child support to have my check garnished.

My daughter Kalah went to Christian College and graduated from Joplin Christian College, and I was proud of her, and Benica because they never gave up and both of them graduated from high school. To see my two daughters march across the stage and get their high school diplomas became one of the proudest moments in my life.

When Benica was placed in a hospital for observation, I visited her and Venita did not want me to speak with the doctor, but her efforts were in vain, and I spoke with the doctor to give a father's viewpoint of what I felt was going on with my daughter, because I studied mental health, when I worked on my Master of Science degree in Counseling Education from Southern Illinois University at Edwardsville, Illinois class of 1975, and could point out some of the weaknesses which probably kept her from functioning properly. Benica told me she wanted to be a writer like me, and I encouraged both of my daughters to practice their writing, because it can help them in any career requiring written communication. To further her education, Benica told me she took correspondence courses. Other events took place, where Kalah and her classmates took trips to Haiti, and she sent me e-mail pictures of what activities they were involved in.

For Father's Day, Kalah and Benica sent me cards saying how much they missed me. To see my house on Maffit Avenue made my daughter Benica proud of me, because I showed her despite how child support came out of my check illegally, I refused to quit my job, and fought in court, to get it lowered. I have not seen my two girls in about nine years, because their mother took them to Colorado without telling me how I could get in touch with them, and now they are grown women. During that time they sent me a photo album showing me how they looked. I miss them and hope to see them again one day. I remember going over to their house and Benica and Kalah danced with each other, and while they did it; they did not think I could keep up with them, but they were surprised; I could dance with them at a fast speed. When they wanted to go places, I received calls to take them, and I never turned them down if I had the time to do it. Venita's car broke down on the highway, and I went to pick her and my daughters up, and when they got out of high school in the evenings when it was over. Both of them were good in music, and I came to one of their concerts, and saw Benica playing in the band. School activities took place in their lives, and I took them out to the school for a sleepover with their classmates, with the students' parents acting as guardians. I asked my daughter why they wore pajamas to school, and they said it was because the students did it too. I visited them when they lived in a big house with many rooms in it. When they needed some school supplies, and I could not buy it, their older brother Dennis bought it for them, because I did the same thing for him when he attended grade school, and paid to send him on trips to Colorado to see his grandparents. Their mother worked and sometimes I stayed at the house and watched them, and they always went into their rooms for privacy. One wonderful experience took place when my son Charles Jr, Kalah, Benica, and me spoke to each other in a three-way telephone conversation. At school, my daughter Benica gave a speech in class, and she said she wanted to be a writer, and teacher like her father, and Kalah wrote me a letter saying that I made her feel she could do anything, because she saw how I kept going to school and earned six academic degrees, and a specialized certificate, and attended Concord on line law school for a year, even though I grew up in the low income areas of the city, and never let anything stop me from my dream of getting a good education. Both of my daughters are very religious and Kalah wanted to go into the ministry. They take their dog with them to many places when going out. I cannot wait to see them again.

Last year a friend of my cousin Eric called him and asked if he knew Michelle's father, who substitute taught in the Jennings School District before, and Eric said he did, and Eric said he was in one of the gym classes I taught. Later Michelle called Eric, and he told her about me. I later called Michelle, and for about a year, we talked on the phone, and later I went out to her mother's house, and Sharon introduced her to her father for the first time of her life. Sharon, and I have remained close friends ever since and communicate with each other constantly, and talk about many topics which interest us. Mick is the name I call my daughter, and she looks just like me. We clash at times because I want her to call me father instead of Charles. If she needs me, I am always there for her but want her to call me what I told her to address me as, when we see each other. The reason I did not stay with her and her mother was because Sharon moved, and I did not know where they were. I visited the church Michelle belongs to and sat beside her in service. It's difficult for her to call me father because she's not use to it. Following her mother's and father's steps, she graduated from Fontbonne University in St. Louis with a Bachelor of Science degree in Business Administration. Sharon has her Bachelor of Science degree and Master of Science degree. I will try to get to know my daughter, but Sharon keeps telling me Mick is stubborn like me. I love my daughter, and her mother very much, and Mick can dance, and cook good meals for dinner.

CHAPTER 24

A TRIBUTE TO A BEAUTIFUL BROTHER BY THE NAME OF TERRY USSERY, WHO TOUCHED THE LIVES OF MANY PEOPLE WITH THE CHRISTIAN LOVE OF GOD

As I approach the Light House Seven-Day Adventist Church located at 4557 San Francisco Avenue, St Louis, MO, as the sun shined so brightly, a gentleman stood in front of the church directing people.

A loud noise echoed within the sanctuary, giving praise and complements to one of their outstanding deacons by the name of Terry Lee Ussery, Jr., who died on November 8th 2012 and when I walked into this beautiful church, Terry's casket sat in the front of the pulpit and other ministers sat in a small area. One of the ministers spoke about Terry's contribution to his church, family, and friends and other people came up to say nothing but positive things about him. When I first worked as a security officer at 4444, a gentleman came up to the front desk and said, "Hello, my name is Terry", with a pleasant smile on his face. I said, "I'm officer Pointer", and we shook hands. Terry said, "I work upstairs in the Genome Sequencing Department and Washington University pays my tuition as a result of me working for them". With both of us having interest in writing, we developed a good relationship with each other. I helped him when he took English composition and gave him advice on improving his paper. Being a Christian and father with three children, two sons Terry Usser, the third, and Joseph Usser, and a daughter, Alyssa Usser. Terry and Sharon, his wife, instilled in their children the value of keeping God in their lives and living a Christian life. Terry Usser, Sr., supported his son's desire to go into the ministry. Even doing the funeral, his wife, Sharon despite her grief sang happily and emotional with the choir. Visitors testified and said Terry was a wonderful person and one speaker said Terry did not care about the distance; he took her home in the time of need. Terry told the young lady to check with his wife Sharon and Sharon told her to check with Terry. One fellow said," Terry was just like a father to me and encouraged me to keep writing my poetry and now it's getting more professional exposure in the literary world". Terry was always interested in the members of the church he served as deacon, men's ministry leader, and consultant at the youth minster for the church. When I asked Terry to write more, he said, "I am too busy trying to get my children in college, church work, and going to school at night." His wife Sharon worked at 4444 Forest Park and sometimes I saw both of them happily holding hands and going to their car to pick up their children from school. One fellow said to the audience, "Terry never talked to people in a sarcastic way and was willing to help anyone that needed help." Terry loved wrestling and discussed this topic with his co-workers and showed much respect to all people. The last speaker was his son who said, "I miss my father, but we clashed on his beliefs, and he told me to get out of his house when I turned eighteen. My father won all the arguments we had as he raised me. You people must get right with God because you don't know when the last time you will be on earth. The last time I saw my father; he visited me at school and said he was proud of me". This is dedicated to a man of God, who set an example of Christian love which he showed to many people who developed a relationship to all races of people who got to know him. Terry told me on November 7, which was the last time I spoke to him before he died on November 8th. He said, "Charles I am going into politics but I want to finish college first". I said to him, "You don't have to finish college to run for political office; you have to find out what you can do to serve the needs of the people". Terry was my friend and most people he knew he touched them in a spiritual way. He had a pleasant personality. When I experienced problems, writing my book, "The Making of a Black Belt Karate Champion", he always stopped at the desk and asked me how it was coming. Terry always encouraged me and I dedicate this story to Terry, his wife and three children.

Writing this book took me through a journey of many memories both good and bad. I hope it will inspire other people to achieve their goals despite the difficulties which stand in their way.

I graduated from Southern Illinois University at Edwardsville in 1974 with a Bachelor of Science degree in Secondary Education, history major, English minor and a Master of Science degree in Counseling Education, 1975.

I wrote an article on the extension to the St. Louis Convention Center
for the <u>Daily Record Newspaper</u>

The 22th Missouri Court of Appeals. I did oral argument on two cases against two assistant attorney generals.

The Salvation Army Shelter
I stayed here trying to rebuild my life, St. Louis, MO

The Julia Davis Library in St. Louis, MO
Did my first book review before an audience on my book called <u>The Making of a Black Belt Karate Champion</u> published in March of 2012. St. Louis, MO

I wrote articles for the <u>St. Louis Sentinel News Paper</u>.

1984-1985 I interned at KMOX Radio and KMOV TV 4.
Julius Hunter supervised television assignments and Bob Humilton
supervised me in writing the evening news for the radio audience.

In the late 1950's, this was the use to be site of the Igoe Projects where my brother and I grew up. Now this area is a large vacant lot with trees and weeds.

A bridge which went through the Mill Creek area connecting
North St. Louis with South St. Lous. I grew up in this area.

Attended this grade school when I was eight or nine years old.
It was located close to the Igoe Projects.

8th Circuit District Federal Court Defeated 9 federal judges who
signed an enbanc order making me comply with eight unconstitutional
measures before filing my petitions after I appealed to the
Eighth Circuit Appellate Court.

I was born at this hospital on March 12, 1950.
Now it is a senior citizen home.

Received Bachelor of Science degree in Criminal Justice in 2001
from the University of Missouri at St. Louis.

Cleveland High School, St. Louis, MO
I taught social studies at that high school from 1976 to 1980 before and after black students were integrated into the school population.

Florissant Valley Community College, St. Louis
Earned an Associate of Arts degree in Paralegal Studies, Class of 2006.

Washington University, St. Louis, MO
Earned a Specialized Certificate in Journalism and Communications, 1984.
Received my Bachelor of Science degree in Journalism and
Communication in June of 1985.

This was the Tenth Street Pool area where we played in the pool on hot summer days. This area is being developed currently. St. Louis, MO

This building was formerly called O'Fallon Technical High School.
In 1968, I graduated from there with a diploma in Commercial Art.

Forest Park Community College
Earned an Associate of Arts degree in Liberal Arts, class of 1971.
St. Louis, MO